PETER HENNESSEY
BOOKSELLER

P.O. Box 393
PECONIC, N.Y. 11958
(516) 734-5650

Vern Perry

Sixteen
98825 Pleasant Hill Drive
Brookings, Oregon 97415

May 4, 1984

The

NORTHERN PACIFIC

Main Street of the Northwest

The
NORTHERN PACIFIC

MAIN STREET OF THE NORTHWEST

A Pictorial History by Charles R. Wood

BONANZA BOOKS - NEW YORK

517R01382

COPYRIGHT MCMLXVIII BY SUPERIOR PUBLISHING COMPANY, SEATTLE, WASHINGTON

This edition published by Bonanza Books
a division of Crown Publishers, Inc.
by arrangement with Superior Publishing Company
a b c d e f g h

Library of Congress Catalogue Card Number 68-26752

Dedication

To my wife Dorothy May—who insists upon seeing a task through to completion— I dedicate this book.

PRINTED IN THE UNITED STATES OF AMERICA

Contents

Introduction

THE HISTORY of the Northern Pacific stretches back over 100 years to its formal beginning, the signing of the charter by President Lincoln in 1864 to build the road from the Great Lakes to the Pacific Northwest. Actually the Northern Pacific had its beginnings long before the charter was signed, in the earlier explorations of the Northwest, particularly the famous 1804-1806 expedition of Lewis and Clark, the route of which the NP largely follows today. The struggle to finance and build the road was a tumultuous one, and through a succession of presidents, the road was finally completed in 1883 by President Henry Villard.

Although the road was completed to Tacoma in 1883 by utilizing the rails of the OR&N along the Columbia River, it was not complete in the sense that the entire route was directly under the ownership of the Northern Pacific, and it remained for President Robert Harris to initiate the action that carried the road across the Cascades for a direct route over its own rails to the western terminus of Tacoma. The story of the building of Stampede Tunnel through the backbone of the Cascades in 1886-1888, and the bitter experience of the road up on the switchbacks that preceded the tunnel is recounted here in some detail.

Finally, for the steam locomotive fan, a selection of over 100 photographs of the steam power of the Northern Pacific is presented. These photographs, representing the best of many fine collections, were acquired over a period of five years, and while not in any sense are they a complete roster of Northern Pacific motive power, they do represent a good cross section with emphasis on the big modern power.

CHARLES R. WOOD
Seattle, Washington   1968

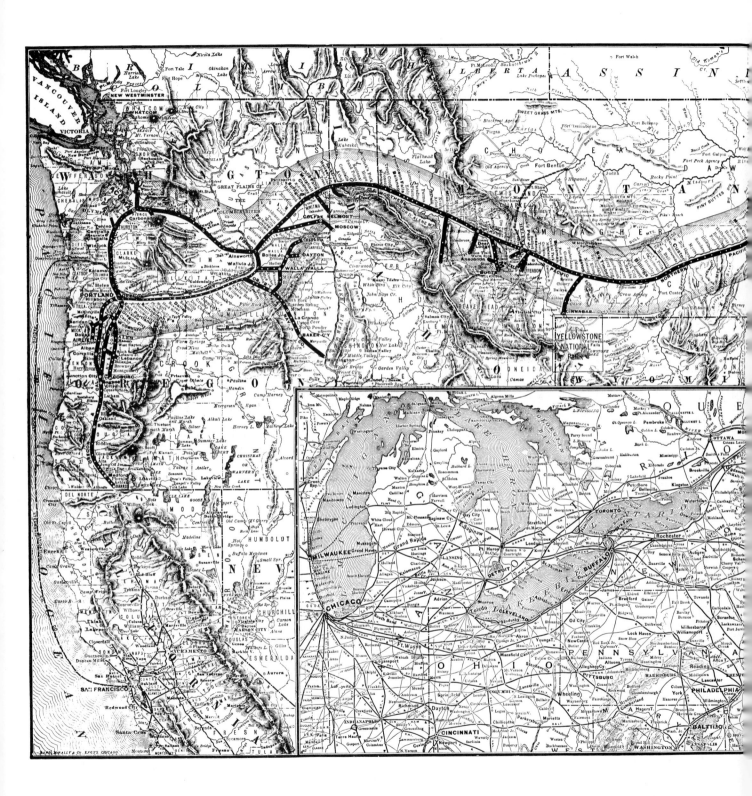

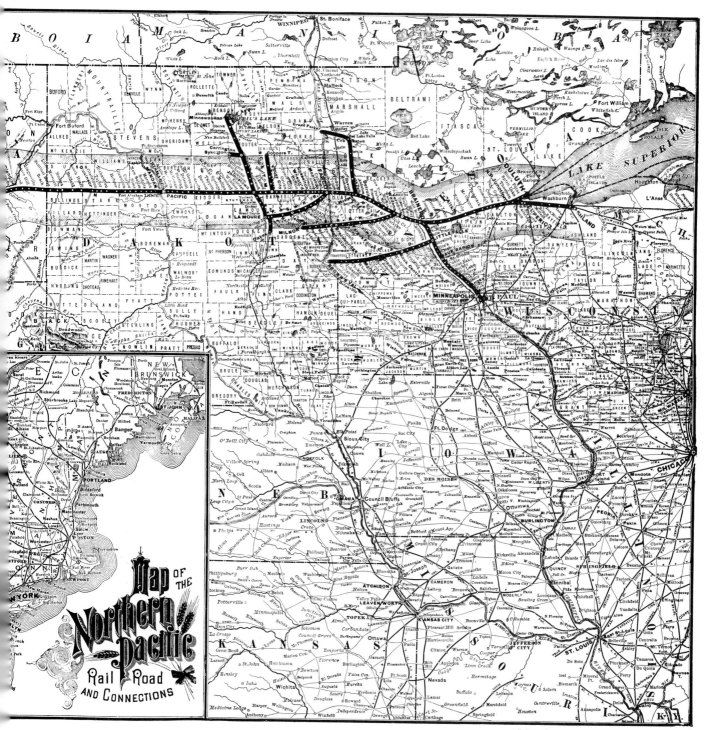

Map from October, 1887 Timetable

Acknowledgments

THE READER WILL recognize that the pictorial history of The Northern Pacific is the work of many individuals, both photographers and collectors of railroad memorabilia. It is to these individuals that both our thanks and credits are given: Ed Nolan, Jack Anderson, Senator Maurine Neuberger, Robert Pearson, Don Roberts, Claude Witt, Willard Wilkinson, Casey Adams, Stan Gray, W. R. McGee, Jim Frederickson, Mike McLaughlin, F. Jay Haynes, Marv Hoskings, Warren Rehberg, J. E. Caron, Bill Wardell, Mike Pearsall, Russ Porter, Wally Swanson, Fred Spurrell, Ron Craig, George Simonson, Stuart Hertz, Bill Converse, Dr. Phillip R. Hastings, and Mr. Bill McKenzie of The Northern Pacific Railway.

A SOLID fruit block roars down the Yakima Valley behind Challenger No. 5137.

Jim Frederickson

8

Chapter I

Exploring A Country And Building A Railroad

In 1964, the Northern Pacific Railway celebrated the 100th anniversary of the signing of its charter by President Abraham Lincoln on July 2, 1864. The signing of the charter was the Federal recognition, and the formal authorization to build the railroad from Lake Superior to Puget Sound, but the steps necessary for building such a road had their beginnings more than three quarters of a century before.

At that time, little was known of the West beyond the Mississippi River, which was the western boundary of the United States. The vast unexplored territory which stretched beyond to the Rocky Mountains belonged to France, and was generally called the Louisiana Territory. Beyond this, in the far Northwest, now the states of Washington, Idaho, Oregon and part of western Montana, the ownership was in dispute, with conflicting claims by Britain, the United States and Russia. As early as 1786, Thomas Jefferson, while serving as Minister to France, tried to arrange a reconnaisance of this country by the American adventurer, John Ledyard. The plan was to explore the Northwest from west to east by way of Russia, Alaska, and the West Coast. Ledyard got as far as east of Kamchatka with Russian permission, when Catherine the Great, suspicious of his real motives, had Ledyard escorted from Russia in a sealed carriage to Poland, with the warning not to return. "Thus failed the first attempt to explore the western part of our continent," Jefferson wrote in his journals years later.

To the British went the honor of being the first to cross the continent north of Mexico, when Alexander Mackenzie, in 1792 traveled from Fort Chipewyan in Northern Alberta, Canada to tidewater, about 100 miles north of Vancouver Island, via the Peace, Fraser and Bella Coola Rivers, laying claim to all these lands for England. Captain Vancouver had already circumnavigated Vancouver Island and explored much of Puget Sound (named for his Second Lieutenant, Peter Puget).

Farther south, the American, Captain Robert Gray, in May of the same year had discovered the Columbia River and Grays Harbor, and laid claim to the surrounding land for the United States. Jefferson's proposal to the American Philisophical Society in 1792, that they underwrite (by subscription) an exploration of the vast, unpopulated region stretching from the Mississippi River to the outlet of the Columbia River (then called the Oregon), met with frustration, and it was not until he became President in 1801, that he was able to begin again to work on a plan to explore the Northwest.

In 1803, with the purchase of the Louisiana Territory from France, and a secret appropriation from Congress, President Jefferson commissioned two Virginians, Captain Meriwether Lewis (his

THIS PORTRAIT OF CAPTAIN MERIWETHER LEWIS, who was commissioned by President Jefferson to explore the Louisiana Purchase, hangs with the portrait of Captain Clark on one wall of Northern Pacific's Travellers' Rest Lounge Car on the Vista-Dome North Coast Limited.

Northern Pacific Railway

private secretary) and Lieutenant William Clark to head an expedition to "explore the Missouri River, and such principal stream as, by its course and communication with the waters of the Pacific Ocean, whether the Columbia, Oregon, Colorado, or any other river may offer the most direct and practicable water communication across the continent for the purpose of commerce." They were to explore the country, observe the growth of vegetable production, and make scientific notes of the climate, the minerals, and animals. They were to establish communication with the Indian tribes, observe and record their customs, laws, and languages, and finally to establish the authority of the United States over this territory and its inhabitants.

In May 1804, the Lewis and Clark expedition set forth in small boats up the Missouri River from St. Louis, and by November, the thirty-five man party had established their winter quarters at the Mandan Indian towns, about 50 miles from the present town of Bismarck, North Dakota. Here the party built Fort Mandan, and resumed their journey up the Missouri, in April 1805, passing the mouth of the Yellowstone

late in the month. Early in June the party arrived at the mouth of the Marias River where it joins the Missouri, north and east of Great Falls, Montana, and there was considerable doubt at this juncture just which river was actually the Missouri. Lewis, on a separate reconnoiter found the Falls of the Missouri, and knew that according to the information given them by the Indians at Mandan, that he was still on the right course. By June 19, the party passed from the east slope of the Rocky Mountains through the Gate of the Mountains near Helena, Montana.

On July 25, the expedition came to the Forks of the Missouri, and renamed them the Jefferson, the Madison and the Gallatin in honor of President Jefferson, Secretary of State Madison, and Secretary of the Treasury Gallatin. These were not separate rivers —the west fork or the Jefferson was the main stream with the others tributary to it. Continuing up the Jefferson River, Lewis crossed the Continental Divide on August 13, and came to a stream whose waters he surmised flowed to the Pacific Ocean. Actually, he had discovered a stream running into the Salmon River, in what is now Idaho. He also discovered the Snake River, but the rapids were too dangerous to permit following it in canoes to its junction with the Clearwater River, at what is now Lewiston, Idaho. Instead the expedition turned north, and proceeded on horses, obtained from the Indians, to the headwaters of the Deer Lodge River, which becomes successively the Hell's Gate, Missoula River and Clarks Fork of the Columbia. On the advice of the Indians, the party then turned west, and pushed over the Bitterroot Range of the Rockies. They constructed canoes on the upper waters of the Clearwater and followed the river to its junction with the Snake River, and by October 17, still following the Clearwater River, they reached the Columbia near what is today Pasco, Washington. Floating down the mighty Columbia, they sighted the Pacific Ocean near Astoria, Oregon on November 7.

After wintering on the coast, the expedition began the return journey on the 23rd of March, 1806. On the way back up the Columbia, Clark discovered the Willamette River, giving it its Indian name, Multnomah. By the first of May the party was back to the Clearwater River in Idaho and pushed on to the fertile and beautiful Camas Prairie home of Chief Joseph and the friendly Nez Perce Indians. They crossed the Continental Divide on May 26th and reached Travelers' Rest near Missoula on Lolo Creek, also exploring the Yellowstone River and Deer Lodge Pass. Going up the Gallatin River, they crossed the Belt Mountains from its east fork through what is now called Bozeman Pass, the route used by the

Northern Pacific, and on September 23 returned to St. Louis after an absence of over two years.

There had been no word of the party since they had left the Mandan Towns in April 1805, and their return was triumphant. They had magnificently achieved their purpose of exploration and establishing the authority of the U. S. over the Indian tribes. Except for brief encounters with the warlike Sioux and Flatheads, the expedition made friends with the Indians, establishing mutual feelings of trust and respect. It remained for succeeding generations to break this trust, losing the friendship of the Indians, and culminating in the savage Indian Wars along the frontier.

In the period following the Lewis and Clark Expedition, the entire territory of Oregon and Washington very nearly became a part of the British Empire due to a lack of interest on the part of the government of the United States, and a very active interest by the powerful Hudson's Bay Company, operating out of its headquarters at Vancouver, Washington on the lower Columbia. The Company had established a trading post at Walla Walla in southeastern Washington, Fort Colville on the upper Columbia, and others on the Spokane and Kootenay Rivers. It had acquired the Canadian Northwest Fur Company, which had previously purchased the interests of the Pacific Fur Company, founded by American, John Jacob Astor in 1811, thus bringing the entire Columbia River area under its influence.

Further east where Americans were trapping and trading up to the eastern slopes of the Rocky Mountains, Army Captain Bonneville, wishing to explore the country further to the west, crossed the Rockies in 1832 with a party of hunters and trappers, coming to the Columbia by way of the Snake River and across the Blue Mountains in Oregon. Thwarted in his efforts to trade with the Indians by Hudson's Bay Company, Bonneville returned to the Army in 1835.

In the same year, Reverend Samuel Parker of Ithaca, New York, after crossing the Rockies with a party bringing supplies to American Fur Company Posts, travelled extensively in Washington and Oregon, exploring the Walla Walla, Palouse and Spokane country, and journeyed down the Columbia to Astoria. Upon his return to the Atlantic Coast, he wrote a book about his travels describing the country and the Indian tribes living there. In this book, he made first mention of a possible railroad to the Pacific Northwest when he wrote, "There would be no difficulty in the way of constructing a railroad from the Atlantic to the Pacific Ocean. There is no greater difficulty in the whole distance than has already been overcome in passing the Green Mountains between Boston and Albany and probably the time may not be

CAPTAIN WILLIAM CLARK, co-commander with Captain Lewis of the Lewis & Clark Expedition, through the Northwest to the Pacific in 1804-1806. *Northern Pacific Railway*

far distant when tours will be made across the continent, as they have been made to Niagara Falls, to see nature's wonders."

In 1836, Dr. Marcus Whitman (who had started for the Pacific Coast with Reverend Parker in 1835, but turned back) again started for Oregon with his wife, Reverend and Mrs. Spalding and W. H. Gray. The Whitman Party joined the American Fur Company trading caravan and crossed the Rockies to Fort Hall, in what is now southeastern Idaho. Against the advice of all at the Fort, Whitman bought a wagon and continued on through to the Columbia, proving that it was possible to bring families and household goods to the region.

By 1840, there were thirty-two missionaries and their families in the territory along the Spokane River and ranging from Walla Walla to the Clearwater in northeastern Idaho. The settling of the Americans did not pass unnoticed. The Hudson's Bay Company, in an attempt to secure possession of the entire Pacific Northwest for its agents moved forty families from Canada to Puget Sound in 1842, and then to the Willamette and Tualatin Valleys in Oregon. It also began fortifying Fort Vancouver, and a British warship was put on station in the Columbia River. Dr. Whitman, fearing that the Americans either would

ISAAC I. STEVENS, Governor of Washington Territory, was appointed by Congress in 1853 to head the survey team exploring the northern route from St. Paul to Puget Sound.

passable only during good weather. Other means of transport, such as river boats, were not only painfully slow, but were restricted to only such towns as could be reached by navigable waters. The railroad then offered a means of opening up the vast distances of the Far West, and Dr. Barlow proposed that the government, using funds from the Treasury, build a railroad at an estimated cost of $30,000,000, with a construction time of about three years. Both estimates were far short of what was actually needed in cost and time, but he was essentially correct in his assertion that such a road would increase trade with the Orient, and provide a bond between East and West.

While Dr. Barlow's letters stimulated some interest in an east-west railroad, the country as a whole was not prepared to act. The U. S. was wrestling with internal problems such as South Carolina's threat to secede from the Union over tariffs, the financial panic of 1837, and the battle for Texas independence, all of which were of greater significance to the average American than the building of a railroad across 2,000 miles of wilderness.

Another who saw an east-west railroad as a means of increased trade with the Orient was Asa Whitney, a wealthy New Englander, who had lived and traveled widely in the Far East. In the summer of 1844 he traveled with a group of adventurers to the headwaters of the Missouri. He studied the country, listing its resources and estimating the land values for possi-

be forced out of their new homes or made to become British subjects, journeyed, in the winter of 1842, across the country to call to the attention of President Tyler and Secretary of State Daniel Webster, the plight of the American settlers. His plea was successful, and in January 1843, a treaty between Great Britain and the United States confirmed all the territory in the present states of Oregon and Washington to the U. S.

Concurrent with Reverend Parker's writing on the possibility of a railroad across the Rockies to the Columbia, Dr. Samuel Barlow of Massachusettes was writing lengthy letters to newspaper editors about the feasibility of a railroad from New York City to the mouth of the Columbia. A well educated and articulate man, his letters were more in the nature of articles then mere "letters to the editor."

Railroads in the U. S. had started to become a practical means of transportation only about 1830, and by 1835 were rapidly expanding with nearly a thousand miles of track in use, mainly on the East Coast, but some reaching as far west as Michigan and Illinois. There was a tremendous need for the railroads for transportation, communication and dependable mail service because the roads in the U. S. were

JOSIAH PERHAM, promoter of the People's Pacific Railroad Company and First President of the Northern Pacific, was the man responsible for the securing of the Northern Pacific Charter, signed by President Abraham Lincoln on July 2, 1864.

Josiah Perham

ble sale in the public domain, with a view toward building a railroad from the Great Lakes, across the Great Plains and the mountains to the Pacific. Convinced that his idea was sound, he returned to Washington, D. C. and proposed that the government grant him lands for thirty miles on either side of the right of way from Lake Michigan to Puget Sound, a distance of 2400 miles. The road built in 6′ gauge, laid with 64 lb. rail and to be completed within 25 years was to be the sole property of Whitney and his heirs, with the government establishing the rates and regulating the operations. Whitney would be paid a salary of $4000 a year to manage the road, and planned to bring in emigrants both to help build the railroad and to create traffic for it, paying them for their labor with land. This would eliminate labor costs, and the material would be paid for out of government funds.

An eloquent and persuasive speaker, he expounded his ideas to any group that would listen. First greeted with skepticism, he eventually won the consideration and approval of influential government officials and representatives who presented his bill to build the railroad before the Public Lands Committee in 1848. The Senate committee reported favorably on the bill, but it was tabled by a 27 to 21 vote, thus spelling finis to his plans. It is quite remarkable that this bill received so much consideration as it would have removed 77,000,000 acres of land from the public domain and created a government sponsored kingdom for Whitney and his heirs reaching from the Great Lakes to the Pacific. By 1852, discouraged, disheartened and impoverished, for he had spent his fortune promoting his plan, Whitney faded from the national scene.

Whitney's torch was taken up by one of the most respected civil engineers of his time, Edwin F. Johnson, Chief Engineer of the Chicago, St. Paul, & Fond du Lac, later to become the Chicago and Northwestern. Johnson had gained national recognition for his surveying of the international boundary from the Connecticut River to the Bay of Fundy. He had discussed many times with Thomas H. Canfield of Vermont (later to become one of the directors of the NP) the possibility of building a railroad to the Pacific, and with Canfield's encouragement wrote a series of articles for Poor's Railroad Journal outlining the feasibility and urging the construction of such a road. The articles bound in book form were shown to Jefferson Davis, Secretary of War.

Davis, an ardent Southerner from Mississippi, like many other Southerners, wanted to see the center of the Federal Government moved to the South, and thus wished to establish a rail route south of the 35th Parallel. He used his influence as Secretary of War to add a survey amendment to the 1853 Army Bill. With the Army making the surveys, the selection of the route would rest with him, and with the railroad built along the southerly route from Mississippi to California, the whole Southwest would fall under the influence of the South, thereby immeasurably increasing its strength in the fight for slavery.

In the spring of 1853, five survey teams were put in the field to survey the country along the 32nd, 35th, 38th, 39th, 41st, 42nd, 47th, and 49th parallels, with Isaac I. Stevens (then Governor of the Washington Territory) appointed commander of the party to survey the northern route leaving from St. Paul. Captain George B. McClellan was appointed commander of the party starting from Puget Sound, and the two were to meet at Colville, Washington Territory on the Columbia River. This distinguished survey party included in addition to McClellan (who was to become Commander in Chief of the Army of the Potomac during the Civil War), Lt. John Mullan (who would build the first wagon road across the Rockies) and Lt. Rufus Saxton (who would become a brigadier general in the Civil War). Stevens would also become a brigadier general, destined to lose his life in the battle of Chantilly in Virginia in 1862. A champion of the Northern Route, his work as Commander of the survey party was outstanding, and his report was later used as a solid basis for the Northern Pacific Railroad's start as a corporate identity.

The Stevens party explored in depth, the country covered by Lewis and Clark, and in addition explored

J. GREGORY SMITH, 2nd President of the Northern Pacific, started actual construction of the NP Railroad at Thomson's Junction in July, 1870.

J. Gregory Smith

IN 1869, THE BRACKETT PARTY shown here leaving Minneapolis along Washington Avenue on its way west, was one of two surveying and exploring teams put into the field by Jay Cooke & Company to determine the value of the land along the projected right-of-way of the Northern Pacific. The reports of these expeditions convinced the Philadelphia banking firm that the land grant of the NP was of great value and offered a legitimate basis for credit.

Northern Pacific Railway

the Coeur d' Alene, the upper Columbia, and the Marias Pass country, although the actual discovery of the Pass was made by John F. Stevens, Chief Engineer of the Great Northern in 1889. Captain McClellan's party working east, surveyed the country between Seattle and the Columbia River, including Snoqualmie Pass, a route which he considered barely practical because of the formidable snowfall necessitating a long summit tunnel.

Stevens' completed report, in 1855, was comprehensive and thorough, stressing the practicality of the route by way of the Valley of the Missouri or the Yellowstone, and recommending that the Bitter Root Range in Montana be avoided by swinging a line further to the north via Lake Pend d' Orielle, then to Spokane. From Spokane the choice was either across the Cascades to Puget Sound, or a route following the Columbia to what is now Portland, Oregon and then north to Puget Sound. He also stressed both in his report and in later articles and speeches the fitness

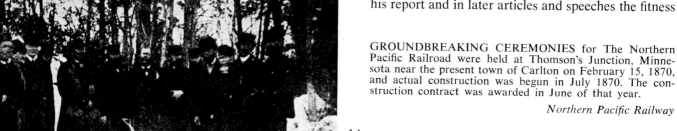

GROUNDBREAKING CEREMONIES for The Northern Pacific Railroad were held at Thomson's Junction, Minnesota near the present town of Carlton on February 15, 1870, and actual construction was begun in July 1870. The construction contract was awarded in June of that year.

Northern Pacific Railway

14

of the entire country for settlement and its suitability for cultivation.

Stevens' report, favorable as it was regarding a northern route, was discarded in favor of the route along the 35th parallel, championed by Jefferson Davis, who emphasized that only this route and one along the 38th parallel would be free of snow in the winter. In addition, California, admitted to the Union in 1850, was extremely vocal in its demands for a railroad running from Omaha to Sacramento, a route closely following the Overland Trail used by the Forty Niners, and with the largest population on the Pacific Coast located here, a central route for the first transcontinental railroad did make sense. The pressure of the Civil War, and the desire to tie the State of California with its loyal northern supporters more closely to the Union, hastened the decision of Congress to grant a charter in 1862 to the Union and Central Pacific Railroads. The extremely generous land grants and the subsidy of Government bonds, coupled with the advantage of being able to issue and sell stock up to $100,000,000 brought the road to rapid completion, with the gold spike ceremony at Promontory, Utah, on May 10, 1869 an occasion of national rejoicing and celebration.

Some Senators from the North, notably those from Michigan, Wisconsin, and Minnesota unsuccessfully attempted to include a subsidy and land grant for a northern railroad in the Union Central Pacific bill. With the death of Stevens, the advocates of the northern route were without a champion, until Josiah Perham, a promoter of successful railroad excursions in the East, and widely known to railway managers and the general public, stepped into the breach. Perham had long dreamed of building a People's Pacific Railroad over essentially the same route chosen for the Union Central Pacific, and had received a charter from the State of Maine to build such a road. He fervently believed that the people of the United States would support his efforts to raise the $100,000,000 necessary to construct the road by stepping forward to buy shares of stock at $100 each, $10 to be paid at the time of subscription. With this in mind, he endeavored to obtain a land grant and subsidy from Congress, but failing in these efforts when the Union Central Pacific Bill was passed, and recognizing a favorable attitude in Congress toward a northern route, proceeded to transfer en masse his friends and entire organization to the northern route enterprise.

Perham made friends with the most powerful man in Congress, Thaddeus Stevens of Pennsylvania, and on his advice, Perham and his associates changed their charter proposal to ask the Government only for a land grant, but twice the amount granted the Union and Central Pacific Railroads, and to rely upon popular subscription to raise the money to build the railroad. Perham dropped the Maine Company charter when Congress objected to a Maine Company building a railroad that was to run from Minnesota to the Pacific, and submitted a new bill on May 23 to create by direct charter the Northern Pacific Railroad Company to run from Lake Superior to Puget Sound. This bill was passed by a House vote of 74 to 50 on May 31st, and on July 2, 1864, having passed both houses of Congress was signed by President Lincoln.

Perham received a land grant amounting to 47,-000,000 acres, and an important amendment to the bill proposed that the titles of land awarded the Indian tribes within the area of the grant were extinguished. He was also authorized to issue $100,000,-000 in stock, but was prohibited from mortgaging either the railroad or the land grant so that construc-

JAY COOKE, financeer without peer, in one of the few known photographs of him in existence, stands at a banquet sponsored by him for eastern stockholders of the company. They journeyed to Duluth, Minnesota in 1871 to celebrate the arrival of the first passenger train in that city and attended the banquet held in the old Emigrant House which stood where the NP freight house now stands.

Northern Pacific Railway

FIRST HEADQUARTERS of the Northern Pacific Railroad were at Brainerd, Minnesota in 1871. Later, general offices were moved to St. Paul. The unusual little engine here in front of the building at Brainerd is an 0-4-0 switcher type with an even more unusual 4-wheeled tender.

Northern Pacific Railway

THE 12-TON MINNETONKA, built in 1870 for $6,700, was the Northern Pacific's first locomotive. Used initially in construction work in Minnesota in 1870 and 1871, it was then shipped to San Francisco by rail and by steamer to the Columbia River for construction service on the west end of the line building from Kalama to Tacoma, Washington.

Northern Pacific Railway

tion bonds could be issued. This coupled with the lack of a government subsidy made it impossible for Perham to start construction. A few people, mostly his friends in the East did buy stock, but in amounts insufficient even to pay for a detailed survey. The original charter called for a construction start by July 2, 1866, but Perham physically exhausted and deeply in debt secured through his friend Thaddeus Stevens an extension of time in Congress and offered a group of eastern financiers his franchise to build the Northern Pacific. They agreed to pay the debts of the Perham organization mounting to $102,000, leaving Perham nothing for his years of effort. He died in 1868, an embittered and broken man.

This wealthy and influential group controlled several important railroads in New England, an express company and other important business concerns, but as New Englanders carried little prestige or influence outside of this region. They elected as their new president J. Gregory Smith, who held no illusions about a million people being willing to put up $100 each. One of his first official moves was to organize an effort to pressure Congress into granting a subsidy to build the railroad. His failure to achieve this in 1866 and again in 1867, convinced him that he needed an organization with broader influence, and to achieve this Smith, in what is known as the Original Interests Agreement drew together twelve subscribers to invest $8,500 each for a share of the "Original Interests." Included in this group were the presidents of the Pennsylvania, Erie, Chicago & Northwestern, and the Pittsburgh Fort Wayne and Chicago, as well as the vice president of the New York Central and the owners of three express companies. The new organization chosen more to put pressure on Congress than to organize the company on a sound business basis, also failed, primarily because the attitude of Congress and the country was firmly against any further concessions to the land grant roads. Smith's offer to return to the public domain all lands granted the Northern Pacific Company located on the south side of the tracks in return for a subsidy or guarantee of bonds was refused.

With time running out, and against formidable opposition, Smith and his associates did manage to secure passage of an act extending the time limit to start construction to July 4, 1870. The completion time was extended to July 4, 1877 (less time than would be needed), and the charter amended to permit the mortgaging of the railroad, its telegraph lines and later the land grant itself. This permitted $100,000,-000 in construction bonds to be issued, and at long

A NORTHERN PACIFIC surveying team pauses for its picture in Dakota Territory in the late 1870's.

Northern Pacific Railway

TOWNS OF FAIR SIZE were built in Montana Territory using only steamboats and wagons to haul material and supplies, and under the impetus of a gold discovery, they grew even without the railroad. Here in Last Chance Gulch, is Main Street, Helena, Montana, as it looked in 1870 after a gold strike, during the Civil War, brought a rush of gold seekers to the Territory.

Northern Pacific Railway

last the railroad had a legal instrument to raise construction funds, and only the problem of finding a company capable of marketing the bonds to the public remained before construction could begin.

This problem was solved in the selection of the great banking house of Jay Cooke and Company to market the bonds and to manage the finances of the Northern Pacific. Jay Cooke and Company was widely known, on both sides of the Atlantic, as a result of its success in selling government bonds during the Civil War. Jay Cooke, in addition to his background in banking and his valuable contacts in high office, also had a flair for promotion on a grand scale. Enthusiastic and optimistic by nature, his one failing was that he made no provision for the inevitable downturns of business.

Although the idea of building a publicly financed railroad across two thousand miles of wilderness seemed to have little merit, Jay Cooke put two survey parties into the field in the summer of 1869. W. Milnor Roberts, in charge of one party, explored the Puget Sound and Columbia River areas, and proceeded eastward to the passes of the Rocky Mountains and the Upper Missouri country. Governor Marshall of Minnesota, in charge of the other party explored the route from Lake Superior westward to the Red River of the North and across the plains of Dakota to the great bend of the Missouri. Even with the problems and costs of mountain construction, Roberts estimated total cost of construction at $85,-277,000 and the reports of both parties convinced Jay Cooke that the valuable land grants would be worth about four times the construction costs, upon completion of the railroad.

The decision to finance the railroad was under advisement for a year before Jay Cooke stated his terms in an affirmative reply to the Northern Pacific. The banking firm would market $100,000,000 in bonds paying 7.3% interest in gold, at par, but would pay the railroad only $88 for each $100 bond sold, and in addition was to receive $200 in stock for each $1000 in bonds sold. Further, Jay Cooke & Company wished to create a land company to manage the town sites, and to become the sole financial agents for the railroad. In effect Jay Cooke & Company became the controlling managers of the railroad, and if all went well, stood to make a profit of around $53,000,-000.

A joint resolution then was passed in Congress, over much opposition, mortgaging the road and its land grant to the holders of the bonds, and the mortgage was filed in the office of the Secretary of the Interior. Also the Columbia River line was to be the main line and the Cascade line, the branch. Finally, the company was given the right to select lands ten miles beyond the limits of the grant for any deficiency in lands included in the grant, effectively widening the land grant in the States to thirty miles on each side of the line and to fifty miles in the Territories.

In the summer of 1870, with the details agreed upon, Jay Cooke & Company plunged into selling the bonds. Advertisements extolling the Northern Pacific's "Fertile Belt" appeared in the large Metropolitan papers, and in thousands of little daily and weekly papers, reaching into every corner of the land. Writers were employed to praise the merits of the Northern Pacific country—the mild climate, the grass of the plains and mountain valleys where stock could range all winter, the vast forests, and the bumper crops of grain and fruit that could be raised. This tremendous advertising campaign began to pay off in spite of sniping by rival railroads, notably friends of the U. P. who also had land to sell and settle, and by the close of 1871, thirty million dollars' worth of bonds had been sold, mostly to small investors in the United States. A plan to sell $50,000,000 worth of bonds to the Rothschilds in Europe had collapsed with the start of the Franco-Prussian War.

GENERAL THOMAS L. ROSSER (seated wearing white hat) and his survey staff posed at Brainerd, Minnesota in 1871. Rosser, an ex-Confederate Army General, was chief construction engineer in the field for the NP and for more than ten years during the main construction period of the railroad. *Northern Pacific Railway*

IN THIS VIEW looking east from the Headquarters Hotel, in the fall of 1876, the town of Fargo, Dakota Territory is shown.

Northern Pacific Railway

Groundbreaking for the Northern Pacific took place at Thomsons Junction, just west of Duluth on February 15, 1870, but the actual construction of the road began in July, 1870. Thomsons Junction was the meeting point of the NP and the newly completed Lake Superior and Mississippi Railroad, also controlled by Jay Cooke & Company, a line which ran between St. Paul and the Jay Cooke speculative town of Duluth, across the Bay of Superior from Superior City, Wisconsin.

For a thousand miles west of Duluth, there was no town or village worthy of the name on or near the railroad. Except for a few traders, military posts, and some Indian agencies, the country between the Red River and the Missouri was in control of the Sisseton and Wahpeton bands of Sioux Indians, who had recently destroyed the settlement of Breckenridge on the Red River. There was not the sort of traffic that a railroad needs for revenue until the gold mining camps in the Rocky Mountains, and such towns as Helena, Bozeman and Deer Lodge, with a combined population of around 20,000, were reached. Along the lower Columbia, the Willamette, and around Puget Sound, there was in the aggregate about 100,000 people engaged in raising wheat, trading and logging. With the largest communities 2,000 miles from St. Paul at the western end of the railroad, it was largely up to the Northern Pacific to create its own markets. In this, the political support and facilities furnished by the communities in Montana, Oregon and Wash-

THE BUFFALO once roamed the Plains in uncounted millions, and provided food and clothing for the Indian tribes. The white men slaughtered them for their hides and left the meat to rot. Their bones were later picked up by half-breed "Buffalo Bone Pickers" and hauled by Red River Carts to the railhead.

Northern Pacific Railway

ington were of inestimable value to the road, even though they were too small to provide capital and labor.

With thirty million dollars in construction funds secured in less than two years, an early completion of the railroad seemed possible. Regular schedules were in operation between Brainerd, the NP headquarters, and Duluth, by the winter of 1870, running over the rails of the L. S. & M. from Thomsons Junction to Duluth. Earlier in the year the NP had bought a controlling interest in the St. Paul & Pacific to eventually give the road direct entry into St. Paul, and on the Pacific Coast, an executive committee from the NP headquarters was locating a line between the Columbia River and Puget Sound. Although the western terminus of the line still had not been chosen, twenty-five miles of line was laid in the Cowlitz Valley between Kalama and Puget Sound to satisfy the charter requirements. The track to Moorhead and Fargo on the Red River was spiked down by the end of 1871, and opened to traffic February, 1872. Survey teams were in the field in North Dakota, Mon-

tana, and in the areas along the Snake and Columbia Rivers.

Then construction funds that had poured in for nearly two years slowed to a dribble, while the NP had started costly construction programs on many fronts. Moving materials on the rails in the East was costly enough, but in the West, with all supplies rounding Cape Horn aboard ships, the freighting bills doubled and tripled. The company had also purchased controlling interests in the Oregon Steam Navigation Company which operated steamboats on the Columbia, Snake and Willamette Rivers and on Puget Sound, and the portage railroads along the Columbia.

The shortage of construction money in 1872, caused by the saturated investors' market, forced many economies on the NP, and construction slowed. A committee composed of Charles B. Wright, Frederick Billings, George Cass and six other members selected Tacoma, on Puget Sound, as the site of the western terminus. President Smith, under fire from other members of the board for what they regarded as his extravagance, resigned in August 1872, and General Cass returned from Puget Sound to take over the presidency in October.

Jay Cooke, in an attempt to bolster confidence in the bonds, would sell $100,000 and quietly buy back $90,000, but these efforts had little effect. A floating debt of over $5,000,000 was embarrassing the com-

THE ROUNDHOUSE at Brainerd, Minnesota housed these wood burning locomotives, as construction forces pushed westward in 1877.

Northern Pacific Railway

pany, and the directors were forced to loan money personally to the company to avoid litigation. On September 18, 1873, Jay Cooke and Company and the Northern Pacific went down together in the financial panic of 1873, the most serious panic since 1837. Warning signals flying since 1872 had been ignored, and the swiftness of the financial disaster caught thousands of investors by surprise. The banking system of the country was paralyzed, and hundreds of thousands thrown out of work. Construction of the railroad halted on the east bank of the Missouri at Bismarck, North Dakota, 450 miles west of Duluth. In the far Northwest, the line from Kalama to Tacoma had been completed, but a single "mixed" per

day was sufficient to accommodate the business generated. The line had no direct connection with Portland, except by ferry, and the Pacific Division as it was known, was nearly 1,500 miles away from the other end of the road on the Missouri River.

Charles B. Wright became president in 1874, when the fortunes of the Northern Pacific were near zero. The company had no credit and the bonds had long since ceased to sell. Trains ran only as far as Fargo during the winter months because, with so little settlement west of Fargo to Bismarck, it was more economical to terminate the operations on the Red River. Trouble brewed in the Northwest where the people of Eastern Washington, impatient with

THE ORIGINAL NORTHERN PACIFIC bridge across the Red River between Moorhead, Minnesota and Fargo, North Dakota was completed in May 1872 and NP service into Fargo begun on June 8, 1872. The need for levees along the river banks is obvious in this photo. During the Spring, melting snow and ice often caused the river to overflow its banks—note the roof of the low lying building showing just above the water to the far left.

Northern Pacific Railway

THE MOST COMMON method of transportation along the Red River of the North, from Fargo to the Canadian border and Winnipeg was by flatboat. Completion of the network of railroad lines serving the Red River Valley in the 1880's put an end to the flatboats, but here near Fargo in 1876, flatboat building still was a big business.

Northern Pacific Railway

construction delay, attempted to take the land grant from the NP through efforts of their delegate in Congress. However, the discovery of coal in the Cascades in 1875, and the construction by the Northern Pacific of a line to the mines at Wilkeson, financed out of the small earnings of the Minnesota and Dakota Divisions, forestalled these efforts.

General Cass acted as receiver of the bankrupt road in the same year, and with a director of the company, Mr. Cheney of Boston, purchased a large amount of land in the Red River Valley, west of Fargo. They employed a successful Minnesota wheat farmer, Oliver Dalyrymple, to manage the Cass Cheney Farm, the first of the "Bonanza Farms." This demonstration of the tremendous wheat production potential of the country resulted in a rapid immigration to the Red River Valley to settle, and furnished traffic for the road.

The reorganization of the railroad in 1875 was accomplished by Frederick Billings, and provided for the bondholders to foreclose on the bonds, take over the property of the company, and issue new stock in the amount of $49,000,000 common stock and $51,000,000 preferred stock. Bondholders received $1,400 preferred or $1,000 common stock in exchange for each $1,000 bond turned in. This exchange of paper for paper caused dissatisfaction and resentment among many, but with no better alternative, the mortgage was foreclosed on August 12, 1873, and by the end of September five sixths of all bonds had been converted. The reorganized railroad was in

possession of nearly 600 miles of road, and ten million acres of land, with a guarantee of three times this amount of land upon completion of the road, and was now in a position to regain the lost public confidence.

During 1876 and 1877, earnings slowly improved. The railroad purchased a controlling interest in St. Paul and Pacific Railroad Company, and completed its line between Sauk Rapids and Brainerd under a new corporation, the Western Railroad Company of Minnesota, for a direct connection between Sauk Rapids, Brainerd and St. Paul. This acquisition and construction corrected a fault of the original charter of the road which had provided only for building from Lake Superior west rather than from the rapidly growing twin cities of Minneapolis and St. Paul.

In 1879, Frederick Billings moved up from his position as one of the directors of the company to succeed Charles B. Wright as president of the Northern Pacific. His first move was to urge that the construction of the railroad be resumed as quickly as possible, since the time limit for completion had expired July 4, 1879 and it was technically possible for Congress to abrogate the charter. Three successive attempts by the company to obtain time extensions from Congress had been effectively blocked by the opposition backed by the Union Pacific. The UP had the only complete line to the Pacific Coast and had no wish to see its monopoly broken. A rider attached to one extension bill would have allowed the Union Pacific construction rights along the Columbia River

BETWEEN 1871 and 1876, construction crews and survey parties in Minnesota, North Dakota and Montana were harassed on numerous occasions by Indian war parties. The fierce Sioux in particular, were greatly feared by settlers and railroad workers, and in 1871, Major General W. S. Hancock ordered out 600 troops to protect survey teams. NP President Smith in 1872 warned U. S. Grant that hostile Indians were slowing construction in Dakota Territory and in 1875 General George A. Custer was assigned to Fort Rice, Dakota Territory to protect the railroad. The climax of the trouble with the Indians was reached in 1876 when on June 25, Custer and his entire command were wiped out at the battle of the Little Big Horn.

General Custer is shown in front of a Northern Pacific tent with some of his scouts. The Indian kneeling beside the General has been identified as Bloody Knife, Custer's favorite scout, who was killed along with Custer at Little Big Horn.

Northern Pacific Railway

that in effect would have blocked the Northern Pacific from reaching the Pacific Coast via the banks of the Columbia. Powerful friends in Washington had advised Billings in 1880 that even though an extension bill could not be passed, neither could a bill be passed cancelling the rights of the Northern Pacific if construction was aggressivey pushed and the road completed by July 1883.

To finance construction Billings devised a plan whereby the company would offer 6% construction bonds in the amount of $20,000 per mile, and to encourage their sale a bonus of $100 in stock was offered with each $100 worth of bonds purchased. In the case of the Pend d' Oreille bonds, this bonus was modified to $70 and work commenced on the Missouri and Pend d' Oreille Divisions in the fall of 1880. Grading was begun in Hell Gate Canyon, west of the Rocky Mountains to block the rapidly advancing grade of the Utah Northern, a subsidiary of the UP, which was moving toward Butte, and in Washington Territory grading was started between Wallula and the Snake River crossing.

With work underway along virtually the entire line, and the successful promotion of $4,500,000 in division bonds, President Billings initiated another

financing plan late in 1880, whereby the entire road and land grant would be mortgaged for $40,000,000. A syndicate of bankers, including the Morgans of the United States and London houses agreed to market the 6% bonds, but under the terms of the loan the bonds could only be issued in amounts of $25,000 for each mile of road completed and approved by government inspectors. The new financing proved an immediate boon, although the inspection procedure was a handicap because the large amounts of money necessary to finance costly bridging and tunneling in advance of the actual track laying could not be obtained. Nevertheless work progressed rapidly, and the new activity served to silence the critics and opposing lobbies in Congress.

In St. Paul construction was started on the new headquarters building, and entrance into Minneapolis and St. Paul was obtained by trackage rights over the St. Paul Minneapolis & Manitoba, although Jim Hill would see to it that no particular advantage would accrue and the NP would eventually have to build its own line into the Twin Cities. Several branches were begun and a smaller road purchased outright along with its land grants.

Sixty thousand square miles of Indian lands,

FROM 1879 to 1882 operation of trains across the Missouri River between Bismarck and Mandan, N.D., was accomplished by laying tracks on the ice in the winter as soon as it would bear the load and by ferry boat when the ice had broken up. The first trip across the frozen-over river was made on February 12, 1879. Even with the light loads imposed upon the ice, which was several feet thick in the dead of winter, passengers and crew members must have felt some qualms when the first train of the winter, to cross the ice, rolled out beyond the shoreline of the "Big Muddy."

Northern Pacific Railway

STEAMBOAT ROSEBUD unloading freight near Fort Benton along the Missouri River in the early 1870's.

NP BRIDGE across the Missouri River.

26

awarded by treaties to the Indians in reservations along the Yellowstone and the Missouri Rivers, were thrown open to settlement by order of President Hayes. The action was justified on the grounds that the Indians rarely used the land and the NP needed it more. The formidable Sioux were in no position to resist this further acquisition, having been subdued in battles with the Army under General Miles and General Crook in 1877, and the friendly Crows submitted to a "purchase" of their land along the Upper Yellowstone for $25,000. Northern Pacific preferred stock rose to $80 a share, the common stock to $50 a share, and confidence in the railroad returned.

With the affairs of the Northern Pacific finally stabilized, the stage was set for the appearance of Henry Villard, emigrant, journalist, financier and President of the powerful and monopolistic Oregon Railway & Navigation Company, the most successful transportation company in the country. The OR&N, since the issue of its first bonds in 1879, had never borrowed a dollar, but raised all its money by selling stock at par to its stockholders. The OR&N, with a vast fleet of modern steamboats and connecting portage railroads, controlled the commerce along the Columbia River, the most important watercourse in the entire Northwest. In 1879, the OR&N had commenced construction of a main line along the south bank of the Columbia River and had also planned a system of feeder lines in Eastern Washington and Oregon. In essence the Columbia River country was the exclusive domain of the OR&N, and Villard planned to keep it that way.

Villard recognized the threat that the NP constituted to his domain, and in 1880, with work on the NP again moving forward, he contacted the executive officers of the NP in order to bring about an agreement that would prevent a head-on collision between the NP and the OR&N. On October 20, 1880, an agreement was reached whereby the Northern Pacific would use the rails of the OR&N along the Columbia River until such a time as the Northern Pacific could complete its own line along the Columbia.

Villard had wanted a permanent agreement, and his next step was an attempt to persuade President Billings to let him raise from ten to twenty million dollars on Northern Pacific first mortgage bonds, feeling that by so doing he would favorably impress the Northern Pacific directors to the point where a permanent agreement for use of OR&N rails would be forthcoming. President Billings, however, was a step ahead of Villard and was already negotiating with other banking firms. When Villard learned of these negotiations, one course of action remained open, outright control of the Northern Pacific.

Villard firmly believed that it was essential to the best interests of both the OR&N and the NP that there be an "identity of ownership." To secure this "identity of ownership," Villard quietly organized his famous "Blind Pool," in February 1881, where trustworthy, wealthy, and influential friends were asked to agree to contribute $8,000,000 for an as yet unannounced purpose. By June 1881, when the new Oregon and Transcontinental Company was formally organized by Villard to create the union of the OR&N

BEHIND THE NORTHERN PACIFIC Depot in Moorhead, Minnesota in the fall of 1876 is the Steamboat Office. Although the railroad crossed the Red River at Moorhead to Fargo, Dakota Territory, it did not, as yet, offer service parallel to it, and the steamboats and flatboats were needed to provide this transportation to points along the river.

Northern Pacific Railway

WHEAT FIELDS in the Red River Valley during the 1870's stretched as far as the eye could see. With yields running as high as 20 to 25 bushels per acre, and no crop failures, bonanza farms and others were booming, and settlers flocked to the land. Shown here in 1876 is John Erickson House—Wheat Buyers, in Moorhead, Minnesota.

Northern Pacific Railway

and the NP, he had more than $20,000,000 available to him to purchase stock to control the Northern Pacific.

President Billings attempted to head off Villard's almost certain control of the NP by assigning the $18,000,000 worth of stock that had remained undisturbed in the company treasury, to the members of the executive board. Litigation by Villard followed to prevent this and on September 15, 1881 a compromise saw a new board of directors that represented both the Oregon and Transcontinental Company and the management of the Northern Pacific. In the board election of 1882, that gave additional representation to the syndicate of bankers who had taken the forty million dollar loan, Villard was elected president, and now had available to him better than $60,000,000 to complete the railroad.

Villard undertook the task and predicted that the

road could be completed within two years, although over 900 miles of mainline remained to be completed. In June 1882, the ends of track were still east of Glendive, Montana and west of Ritzville, Washington. In February, 1882 there had been an unsuccessful attempt in Congress to take away the Northern Pacific land grant because the road had not been completed, and while this bill failed to pass, Villard was well aware that there would be further attempts, and moved to complete the road as quickly as possible. On the western district, thousands of Chinese were brought in to serve as laborers, while Mormons from Utah took subcontracts to grade, and the veteran Swedes and Irish on the eastern end pushed the track ahead. During the two years between September 1881 and August 1883, the track gangs averaged a mile and a half per day.

Problems were encountered in construction, particularly in the mountains of Montana. After following the long tangents and easy grades, that characterized the NP line from St. Paul, 1,008 miles east, the profile abruptly changed as the railroad encountered the high ridge of the Belt or Bridger range west of Livingston. The charter of the road called for grades no stiffer than 116' to the mile, and although Bozeman Pass made a depression through the Belt Range, it was necessary to bore a 3,610' tunnel at an elevation of 5,557' to maintain this grade. The mountain side of the eastern approach to Bozeman Tunnel was composed of sticky blue clay that continually slid back into the excavation. One slide in July, 1882, filled up a cut that had taken four months to excavate, and all efforts to keep the cuts open were of little avail, until the Gallatin County Treasurer suggested to the division engineer that hydraulic mining methods be employed to sluice away the clay. This method was adopted, and in twelve days, over 8,000 cubic yards of earth were washed away. By October 28th the portal was opened.

Tracklaying, during the winter of 1882-1883, progressed so rapidly that it was necessary to shovel snow off the grade so that work could continue. On March 14 the town of Bozeman was reached, a week ahead of schedule, and the first passenger train arrived March 21. The citizens of the Gallatin Valley had waited many years for the railroad, and celebrated its arrival with a giant banquet.

In June of 1883, the division was completed to Helena. The Rocky Mountain Division, extending 274 miles west of Helena, encompassed some of the most difficult terrain the Northern Pacific faced in completing the mainline to the Pacific Coast. The tremendous trestle constructed over O'Keefe's Canyon was 112' high and over 1,800' long, and another trestle over Marent's Gulch was 226' high and 860' long. Other heavy and spectacular construction included the track through the Coriacan Defile west of Missoula, and the 130 miles of heavy rock work along the Clarks Fork Division.

Also included in the heavy construction necessary, was the Mullan Tunnel that pierced the main divide of the Rocky Mountains. Preliminary surveys in 1871 and 1872 disclosed fifteen passes over the main divide where it would be practical to build a railroad. The choice narrowed to three—Mullan, Little Pipestone and Deer Lodge. Chief Engineer Roberts selected Deer Lodge because, although it lengthened the route by 40 miles, it required no summit tunnel, but his successor, General Adna Anderson changed the location to Mullan Pass. Its location was approved by the Board of Directors in 1881, and work started in December 1881, although final approval of its location was not given by the Interior Department until May, 1883. Expectations that the 3,850' tunnel would be completed in short order because of the solid hard rock encountered at the east portal and through a 700' central shaft to the tunnel level, vanished when soft treacherous rock was encountered at the west portal. It was necessary to timber almost the entire length of the tunnel and to bypass it tempo-

A STEAMBOAT moves up the Red River beside the Moorhead, Minnesota and Fargo, Dakota Territory levee in 1879. On the Fargo side spreads the Grandin Line, a bonanza farm so large that the owners operated their own grain elevator and steamboats.

Northern Pacific Railway

rarily by a track with 18 degree curves and 4% grades to accommodate the first through trains in September, 1883.

On August 23, 1883, the east and west rail crews met in Hell Gate Canyon, 55 miles west of Helena, and Villard scheduled an elaborate spike driving ceremony for September 7 at Gold Creek, Montana. Invitations to attend, at Northern Pacific expense, were sent to titled nobility and V.I.P.'s from Europe, as well as congressmen, senators, ex-presidents, bankers, generals and newspapermen from the U. S. Four special trains, equipped with the best cars the Northern Pacific owned, carried the dignitaries from the East to the site at Gold Creek, and along the way the trains were met in towns gaily decked with bunting and flags by enthusiastic crowds of well-wishers. Some criticism was directed at Villard for the heavy costs of the lavish ceremony, but he had planned to use the important dignitaries as promoters of the Northern Pacific lands.

Two minor accidents served to delay the trains. A rail turned over on a sharp curve on Bozeman Pass coming out of Livingston and set the equipment on the ground, and just beyond Helena, in Greenhorn Gulch, on a temporary track with a 4% grade, a coupling broke, ramming the first section backwards into the closely following second section. Some dignitaries were shaken up, but no one was hurt.

Finally, a day late the four eastern sections pulled into Gold Creek. A thousand feet of railroad had been left unfinished, although contruction trains had moved around the gap on a temporary shoofly.

A thousand people gathered in the special pavilion erected for the ceremony by the gap in the rails, and the Fifth Infantry Regiment played. There were speeches by ex-President Billings, Villard, Governors

AN NP GRADING CREW works in the Big Cut, Beaver Creek Valley, in western North Dakota, 1879.

Northern Pacific Railway

AN NP GRADING CREW is shown working on a fill for the main line right-of-way, in western North Dakota in 1879. Their camp is shown in the background.

Northern Pacific Railway

of the States and Territories, and by ex-President Grant, who rose to popular acclaim.

Finally, the rails were run out on the ties as the band played, and spikes were swiftly hammered into place until just one remained to be driven. The last spike was not a golden spike, but the first spike hammered down at Thomsons Junction, fourteen years before. It was displayed, set into place, and then hammered down in turn by Mr. Davis, who had done the same honors at the first spike ceremony. Mr. Villard, Mr. Billings, General Grant, Secretary Teller, and, finally, for the finishing blows Mr. Davis again. The Northern Pacific was complete from St. Paul to Portland to Tacoma.

USING ONLY HAND TOOLS, mules, horses and wagons, the NP construction crews made amazing progress, and the railroad marched steadily west. Here, in 1879, grading crews work in the Big Cut in Sweet Briar Valley in western Dakota Territory.

Northern Pacific Railway

DUE TO A LABOR SHORT-AGE following the Civil War, it was necessary to import 15,-000 Chinese to help build the western end of the NP railroad. The Chinese along with 10,000 white laborers, primarily on the eastern end, completed the NP on September 8, 1883.

Haynes photo for the
Northern Pacific Railway

THE GATLING GUN BATTERY at Fort Abraham Lincoln in North Dakota, located close to Mandan and the Mandan Indian villages, was designed to impress the Indians with its rapid rate of fire. The Gatling design was a somewhat crude but effective predecessor of the modern machine gun.

Northern Pacific Railway

THIS 1880 PHOTO shows NP work crew building grade and laying track in western Dakota Territory.

Northern Pacific Railway

THIS PICTURE OF OLD NIG, the "Iron Horse" of early construction days, was made near the present site of Miles City, Montana, in 1881 when the Northern Pacific was building its main line from the Great Lakes to Puget Sound. Old Nig took part in the last spike celebration at Gold Creek, Montana two years later, when the line was completed on September 8, 1883.

Northern Pacific Railway

BEFORE THE COMING OF THE RAILROAD, transportation on the Missouri River was largely in the hands of steamboats operating from St. Louis as far upriver as Fort Benton, Montana Territory (near Great Falls). The first through steamboat to Fort Benton arrived in 1860 and by the end of the Civil War (five years later) Fort Benton counted seventy arrivals. By 1890, the steamboat era had ended, finished by the Northern Pacific offering faster, cheaper and more frequent service.

Northern Pacific Railway

THE GATES of the Rocky
Mountains, Missouri River, near
Helena, Montana.

AN NP LOCOMOTIVE UNLOADS a string of cars from the Missouri River "Railroad Transfer" ferry near Bismarck, Dakota Territory in this circa 1880 photo. Although the railroad was operating into Livingston, Montana Territory, construction economies had forced delays in building the expensive Missouri River bridge, necessitating the car ferry in the summer and rails laid on the ice in the winter to connect the two ends of its track.

Northern Pacific Railway

Iron Ore Docks at Ashland, Wisconsin.

SERVICING FACILITIES at Missoula in 1883, rather than being housed in a large multi-stall roundhouse were instead housed in seven separate stalls or buildings, possibly for fire prevention. The locomotives visible are all American (4-4-0) types.

Northern Pacific Railway

UPON COMPLETION of the NP bridge across the Missouri River at Bismarck, N. D. in October 1882, it was tested for strength by loading one span with eight American type locomotives aggregating 560,000 lbs. The bridge passed the test and was deemed safe by the engineering department for any train, with any combination of motive power bringing to an end nearly 10 years of ferry boat operation in the summer and rails laid across the ice on the river during the winter.

Northern Pacific Railway

Coal Docks at Superior, Wis.

THIS PICTURE made in 1876, shows the Missouri River terminus of the NP near Bismarck, Dakota Territory. Freight was transferred to river steamers here, for the frontier ports and settlements in Montana along the upper Missouri and Yellowstone rivers.

Northern Pacific Railway

THE BEAUTIFUL LITTLE 4-4-0 American type was the standard freight and passenger power on the Northern Pacific for many years. This photograph (probably by Haynes) was taken at Fargo, Dakota Territory in 1883.

Northern Pacific Railway

OLD PHOTOGRAPH taken in August 1888 shows the site of the original depot in Tacoma, Washington and the piers used by the railroad for transhipment of merchandise to other Puget Sound ports, British Columbia, Alaska and the Orient. Until the completion of the Northern Pacific in 1883 — via the Oregon Railway & Navigation Company to Portland—the commerce of the Northwest was largely dependent upon large ocean going vessels sailing from California and the East Coast with smaller ships sailing between Puget Sound Ports, and a large fleet of steamboats operating on the great rivers of the Northwest; the Columbia, the Willamette, the Snake and the Fraser.

*Collection of
Jim Frederickson*

THE FERRY BOAT TACOMA was launched at Portland May 17, 1883 after being brought out from New York in 57,159 pieces on board the American ship Tillie E. Starbuck. Three hundred thirty-eight feet long, forty-two feet across the beam and drawing over eleven feet of water, she was the largest steamer launched in the Northwest in 1883, and was used to transfer NP trains across the Columbia River between Kalama, Washington and Goble, Oregon.

*Collection of
Jim Frederickson*

THIS PHOTO taken in the 1880's presents a deck view of an N.P.R.R. ferry with both a freight and passenger train loaded aboard for transfer from one side of the Columbia to the other. Note the odd wheelhouse built on the bridgelike superstructure of the ferry. The ferry is not identified, but is not the Tacoma, as the Tacoma had a centrally located wheelhouse and a much larger superstructure.

*Collection of
Jim Frederickson*

HENRY VILLARD, was president of the Northern Pacific Railroad in 1883, when the first transcontinental line in the Northwest was completed, linking Lake Superior with Puget Sound.

Northern Pacific Railway

SEATTLE SALUTED the newly completed Northern Pacific on September 14, 1883 six days after the ceremony at Gold Creek, Montana with a huge parade and barbecue. Hundreds of guests from Europe and the East rode "last spike" special trains from St. Paul to Tacoma to attend. Seattle, although considerably larger than Tacoma, still did not have a direct connection by rail with Tacoma, the western terminus, and Villard's guests came from Tacoma to Seattle on the steamer Eliza Anderson.

Northern Pacific Railway

GUESTS AT THE BARBE-CUE, on the University of Washington campus September 14, 1883, given in honor of the completion of the Northern Pacific, were treated to 250 bushels of steamed clams, a whole barbecued beef and salmon cooked by Indians in traditional fashion using willow grills.

Northern Pacific Railway

CROW INDIANS GATHER at the site of the "Gold Spike" ceremony on September 8, 1883 at Gold Creek, Montana not far from the town of Garrison. The Indians must have wondered at their fate. Confined on reservations, with buffalo nearly extinct, the white man's iron rails now ran through what had been their country.

F. Jay Haynes

THE VILLARD "GOLD SPIKE" EXCURSION.

LAST SPIKE PAVILION at Gold Creek, Montana was erected by the Northern Pacific solely for this ceremony. Henry Villard, then president of the road, was well aware of the value of publicity and promotion. He successfully planned this ceremony to outshine any other railroad completion, and the NP ceremony stands unique in the annals of railroad history. Shortly after the ceremony, through passenger service was begun between St. Paul and Puget Sound, with the Pacific Express (westbound) and the Atlantic Express (eastbound).

Northern Pacific Railway

THIS MEMORIAL SIGN put up by the Northern Pacific at Gold Creek, Montana commemorates the spot where the last spike was driven on September 8, 1883.

Northern Pacific Railway

THE FIRST GOLD discovered in Montana was at this spot on Gold Creek in 1852, and here close by thirty-one years later, in 1883, the last spike was driven to complete the transcontinental line of the Northern Pacific Railway.

Northern Pacific Railway

BUNTING AND STRIPED PAPER decorate the depot and locomotive at Mandan, Dakota Territory in 1883, as the crews and townspeople await the arrival of the four "Gold Spike" trains from the East on the way to Gold Creek, Montana, September 1883.

Northern Pacific Railway

ONE OF THE FOUR "Gold Spike" specials at Gold Creek, Montana September 8, 1883.

Northern Pacific Railway

THIS 1885 PHOTOGRAPH of Main Street, Helena, Montana Territory, was taken from the NP station. The solid looking brick building on the right is "The Elite" hotel, while further down the street cheaper accommodations advertise rooms and meals at 25c each. Across the dirt street is the "California House" and a rather decrepit "Montana House" beyond. In the middle of the block, immediately behind the Elite is a "Brewery Saloon" where frontier thirsts could be satisfied without the necessity or benefit of aging the potent brew.

Collection of Ed Nolan

THE WATER TANK at Ashland, Wisconsin, the eastern extremity of the Northern Pacific Railroad on Lake Superior east of Duluth, Minnesota, is under construction in this 1885 photograph.

Northern Pacific Railway

THIS PHOTOGRAPH of a Northern Pacific 4-4-0 was taken in Fargo, North Dakota on the Red River of the North, probably in the late 1870's, by F. Jay Haynes. Haynes, a pioneer photographer, followed the frontier west with his camera by foot, horse, rail and canoe through the Dakota, Montana, Idaho and Washington Territories. He was a most remarkable photographer, skilled technically, adventurous, and able to capture the frontier at work. In this photo of engine No. 340 the lack of any shadows indicates that this is an overcast day, yet the lighting on the boiler is full of highlights and crisp detail. The background has gone soft and slightly out of focus, as it should, to make the engine stand out from its background. The curious bystander in the background adds a touch that keeps this from being "just another engine picture."

Northern Pacific Railway

THE ST. PAUL & DULUTH R.R. train is shown at Pine City, Minnesota in 1883. This line was leased by the Northern Pacific to provide a link between Duluth and the Twin Cities of Minneapolis-St. Paul. Later the line was purchased outright by the Northern Pacific.

Collection of Ed Nolan

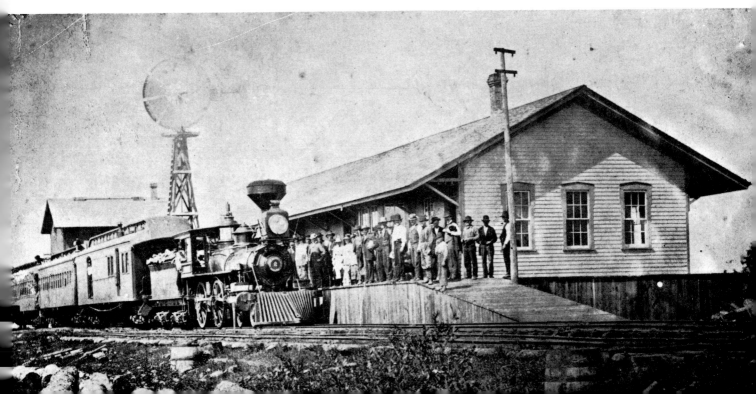

EUROPEAN AGENCY

OF THE

Northern Pacific Railroad,

No. 20 WATER STREET,

LIVERPOOL.

A. ROEDELHEIMER, Agent.

Full and accurate information furnished concerning lands, prices, cost of travel, and openings for farmers, mechanics, tradesmen and, laborers in the New American Northwest.

Illustrated Pamphlets, Circulars and Maps sent free to all parts of Europe on application by post to the Agent.

All persons who contemplate emigrating to America should address

A. ROEDELHEIMER,

20 Water Street, Liverpool, England.

DURING THE PRESIDENCY of Henry Villard a vigorous program of promoting immigration to the Northwest was begun. He established 831 local immigration agents in the United Kingdom and 124 agents in continental Europe. Their efforts were remarkably successful and resulted in thousands of emigrants to the Northwest. Reproduced here is a handbill advertising establishment of the NP European Immigration Agency in Liverpool May 3, 1882.

Northern Pacific Railway

THE FALLS of St. Anthony, from the Stone Viaduct across the Mississippi.

NORTHERN PACIFIC'S first North Coast Limited inaugurated in April 1900, was also the first entirely electric lighted train to serve the Pacific Northwest. Viewed here is the interior of the observation lounge car.

Northern Pacific Railway

Silver Mine and Mill at Butte, Montana.

THE FIRST PASSENGER TRAIN into Minnewaukon, Dakota Territory stands at the station on August 10, 1885. Minnewaukon is on the branch line from Jamestown leading north to the Canadian border town of Leeds. The branch was one of many serving as feeders to the main line planned during the presidency of Henry Villard.

Northern Pacific Railway

Lake Pend d'Oreille, Idaho.

"WOODED UP," NP No. 28 is ready to leave on another assignment from Claymont, Minnesota in 1884. The ubiquitous "American type" of locomotive was well named, for no other locomotive in history was so widely used as the little 4-4-0's. For over a century, burning wood, coal, pine knots, oil or most anything combustible, they travelled main line and branch in all sections of the country from New England to California and from Washington to the Deep South.

Northern Pacific Railway

PULLED BY A FAST STEPPING ten wheeler, an eight car North Coast Limited, train No. 1, charges across the Yellowstone River just east of Livingston, Montana shortly after its inauguration in 1900.

Collection of W. R. McGee

NORTHERN PACIFIC R.R.
Bridge over the Columbia River
at Pasco, Washington.

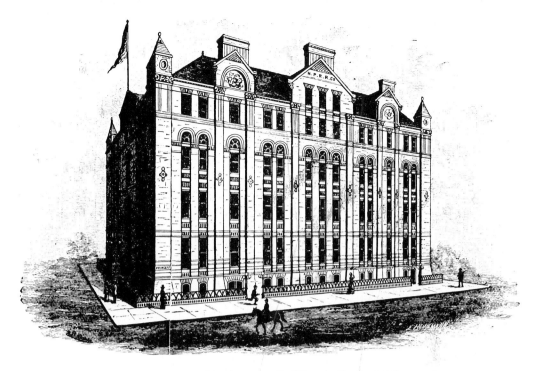

First N.P.R.R. Headquarters Building in St. Paul, Minn.

The N.P.R.R. General Office Building in Tacoma shares this scene with Mt. Rainier in 1890.

Northern Pacific Railway

WASHINGTON TERRITORY VIEWS.

Hadley, Photographer.

A NORTHERN PACIFIC switcher pushes loaded coal cars out onto the coal dock in Tacoma in the late 1880's. Coal from the mines at Wilkeson, Carbondale and Newcastle fields provided considerable traffic and revenue for the Northern Pacific before the turn of the century.

Collection of Jim Frederickson

LOADING LUMBER at Tacoma in the 1880's.

JUST VISIBLE above the roof of the Northern Pacific Freight Office in Tacoma in the late 1880's, is the Sperry Flour Mill with the Pacific Cold Storage Company in the background.

Collection of Jim Frederickson

PICTURED HERE is N.P.'s "Half Moon Yard" in Tacoma not long after completion of the main line across the Cascades in 1888. Although a bigger facility in Tacoma now handles most of the traffic, Half Moon Yard still exists and is in service in 1968. To the right of the photograph is the old N.P.R.R. General Office Building constructed in the 1880's.

Collection of Jim Frederickson

THIS HISTORICAL traveling exhibit car of the 80's and 90's was used by the Northern Pacific Railway to advertise products of the Northwest to prospective homesteaders in the East. C. W. Mott was the general immigration agent at the time, and D. M. Stewart was the traveling immigration agent in charge of this car, which was destroyed by fire while at Elkhart, Indiana in 1898.

Northern Pacific Railroad

THE DEPOT at North Yakima, in Eastern Washington in the early 1900's, has two through passenger trains occupying the main line. Yakima, about 150 miles from Seattle, in the heart of the Yakima Valley, has long been of considerable importance to the Northern Pacific as thousands of carloads of apples and other fruit originate here for shipment east and west.

Collection of Jim Frederickson

THE PE ELL, Washington depot is pictured in 1891 after completion of the branch line to Raymond and South Bend on Willapa Harbor. Located in the heart of some of the finest forest lands in western Washington, Pe Ell was widely known as a prime supplier of Western Union telegraph poles and crossarms.

Collection of Jim Frederickson

A WAYSIDE STATION in 1922 at Martins Bluff (near Kalama, Washington) is decorated with colored posters advertising performances by John Philip Sousa—"The March King"—and his band. Small wayside shelter stations were still numerous on the NP in the 1920's, particularly so on the First Subdivision of the Tacoma Division between Tacoma and Portland, Oregon, originally known as the Pacific Division.

Collection of Jim Frederickson

THE FAMOUS McKinley Stump, from which President Theodore Roosevelt spoke at Chehalis, Washington in 1903, was from a giant fir tree 300 feet tall cut near Pe Ell, Washington on the Willapa Harbor Line in 1901.

Northern Pacific Railroad

THE NORTH COAST LIMITED meets a two car local train spotted on the station house track at Garrison, Montana.

Northern Pacific Railroad

A FREIGHT TRAIN CREW in Auburn, Washington in 1912 poses with their equipment. Of special interest is the rail spiked directly to the ties without benefit of tie plates—a common practice before the advent of heavier locomotives and rolling stock.

Collection of Ed Nolan

FRANCES, WASHINGTON on the Willapa Harbor Line in 1912, could hardly be called a thriving metropolis, but it was a fine example of the many little logging communities that sprang up along the branches of the Northern Pacific throughout Southwest Washington. A footnote in an NP employees' timetable of 1915 referred to Frances in this way, "Log trains between Raymond and Frances will handle adult male passengers when provided with proper transportation".

Collection of Jim Frederickson

AN NP PASSENGER TRAIN pulls into the depot at Granite Falls, Washington in 1909. Granite Falls was once on the old Everett & Monte Cristo Railway line built in 1893 to serve the mines in the Monte Cristo area. The Railway failed in 1900, but continued sporadic operation under receivership until September 1902 when a controlling interest was purchased by the Northern Pacific. In 1915 operations were turned over to the Hartford and Eastern Railroad controlled by the Rucker Brothers. Since the mines were played out, the line was needed mainly to bring out timber, and a limited schedule was operated until the final abandonment of the road in 1925. Today only a short segment of the original 42 mile long branch remains. This spur, running from Hartford to Granite Falls, and again owned by the NP, is used occasionally to serve lumber interests in the Granite Falls area.

Collection of Jim Frederickson

THIS 1909 PICTURE at Lewiston, Idaho shows a period of transition in transportation, with horse drawn vehicles, early automobiles and a train. The locomotive is a Northern Pacific Class F-4 engine, which was scrapped in 1926. Originally built by the Grant Locomotive Works in 1887 for the Montana Union Railroad for $4,632.00, it was acquired by the NP along with the Montana Union Railroad on March 31, 1898.　　　*Northern Pacific Railway*

LOCATED JUST WEST of the Montana line along the Clarks Fork River, Hope, Idaho was once an important division point on the Northern Pacific Railroad. Visible in the far right of the photograph is an old "Armstrong" turntable that must have caused a crew no small amount of effort while turning locomotives, particularly on cold winter nights.

Collection of Robert Pearson

PROBABLY the most unusual engine on the Northern Pacific in 1909 was a geared locomotive, the Heisler, with its tall water tank mounted saddle fashion on top of the boiler. Paired with the more conventional appearing Shay it was used on the Yacolt branch to bring logging trains out of the woods.

Collection of Jim Frederickson

THE CREW POSES with their 0-6-0 type switcher in Third Street Yards in Saint Paul, in 1888.

THE INTERIOR VIEW of the
Everett, Washingon station and
scale house is shown in 1909.
Surprisingly, this station — and
the scale — are still in service in
1968. Telegrapher O. M. Eko
seated at the far right, crippled
all his life, rendered outstanding
service to the Northern Pacific
from July 1905 until his death in
1959.

Collection of Ed Nolan

THE LITTLE LOGGING TOWN of Frances, Washington
has undergone considerable change since its booming days
of 1912, when prime quality timber covered the surrounding
hillsides. In the 1950's, its passenger service was reduced to a
once a day mixed train, and the depot has become nothing
more than a shelter hut for the infrequent passengers.

Jim Frederickson

THE LITTLE TOWN of Yacolt, at the end of the Eighth
Subdivision of the Tacoma Division, about 30 miles from
Vancouver, Washington was important enough in 1912 to
rate a mixed train daily in addition to its daily passenger
service. The scheduled daily train covered the subdivision at
an average speed of 21.5 miles per hour, while the mixed
covered the same distance at an average speed of 8.7 miles
per hour. Here, with Mogul 153 on the head end, the daily
mixed prepares to leave Yacolt at 12:30 p.m. If all goes well
it will arrive at Vancouver Junction—26.8 miles away—at
3:35 p.m.

Collection of Jim Frederickson

THE FIRST NORTH COAST LIMITED with a Schenectady built ten wheeler on the point, hustles along the main line in 1900. Scheduled running time westbound between St. Paul and Seattle was 62 hours 30 minutes. Intended as a summer only service, the public acceptance of the train put it on a year around schedule by 1902.

Northern Pacific Railway

A PASSENGER TRAIN CROSSES over one of the tremendous trestles along the North Pacific's Coeur d' Alene line near Dorsey, Idaho about the turn of the century. The photograph was taken following the rebuilding of the bridge destroyed by a forest fire in 1895, evidence of which can be seen on the hill in the background.

Northern Pacific Railroad

PHOTOGRAPHED at White-hall, Montana in 1898, Mogul No. 555 is equipped with an experimental cinder return on the stack. The little 2-6-0 was one of several NP locomotives fitted with this device. The experiment — moderately successful — led eventually to the development of the cyclone front end that effectively controlled cinder emission.

W. R. McGee

BEHIND A LONG BARRELED and high wheeled American type an NP "Short Line" passenger train poses at New Duluth Station in 1892.

Northern Pacific Railway

THE CONDUCTOR and brakeman dressed in their Sunday best and smoking "five for" cigars pose beside their caboose at Auburn, Washington in the early 1900's. The caboose, big for a 1900 era "bobber," also served as a carrier of less than carload freight as is evident from the large side door, through which goods were delivered to consignees along the line. Typical of NP cabooses is the deeply arched roof, lack of end windows (through which an unwary trainman could be thrown when the slack action was particularly violent) and the generous cupola. The frail looking wooden beamed archbar trucks caused more than a few accidents when a strap broke and snagged a switchpoint or frog, and their fragile construction was one of the primary reasons they were later outlawed by the I.C.C. for interchange service.

Collection of Ed Nolan

A SPOKANE PORTLAND & SEATTLE freight train with one of the high stepping GN design Atlantic types on the head end stands beside its crew. The SP&S was first known as the Portland & Seattle Railway when it was constructed along the north bank of the Columbia River between Pasco and Vancouver, Washington by the NP and the GN. Motive power of the SP&S has always been unique in that it is a blend of both NP and GN designs and, except for the road name, it is impossible to tell the engines apart from their GN and NP counterparts.

Claude Witt

IN THE CALM after the storm, a rotary attacks drifts near Guptil, North Dakota in 1907. People who have not lived out on the plains of the Dakotas and Eastern Montana have little conception of the fierceness of a blizzard roaring in out of the north. The temperature can drop many degrees to sub zero in just a few hours, as a cold front moves in on an icy wind that picks up fallen snow and drifts it as high as a two story house, plugs railroad cuts and low spots, and sweeps the higher areas bare to the frozen ground. The snow is so fine and dry that it will blow through a keyhole making a little drift like white sawdust on the floor, while frost and ice trace infinite patterns on storm windows. Trains run late, if at all, and extra heater cars are assigned to transcontinental passenger runs. Lavatory drains freeze solid under the Pullmans and coaches and it is a losing battle to reopen them with live steam at station stops. A rugged country—these Dakotas—during the winter time, and it took equally rugged people from Scandinavia and Northern Europe to settle it.

Collection of Ed Nolan

IN THE 1920's ENGINEER John Henry Benson oils around his Pacific type locomotive. The white mustached aristocratic appearing old gentleman started pulling a throttle on the NP in the 1870's and retired in the 1920's after a half century of service.

Collection of Ed Nolan

ENGINES SUCH AS THIS American type at Sopena (Vader), Washington in 1912 once saw wide service on the NP, handling everything from main line assignments to the most menial of branchline chores. They gave a good account of themselves over the more level districts in 1870's and 1880's, but as train weights rapidly increased after the completion of the main line in 1883, they were relegated to lighter service and replaced by Moguls, Prairies and light Consolidation types.

Collection of Ed Nolan

WITH AN ELDERLY American type leading, and a 4-6-0 running as road engine, the North Coast Limited pounds through Sandpoint, Idaho, where the crossing of Lake Pend d' Oreille involved building the most extensive trestlework on the entire Northern Pacific. A pile bridge 8,400′ long was constructed across one arm of the deep lake into Sandpoint, and west of the town three more pile bridges varying from 1,300′ to 2,000′ in length were constructed.

Collection of Robert Pearson

ON THE OREGON SIDE of the Columbia River, Union Pacific's eastbound Pacific Limited whistles for the new station at Bonnneville erected by Army engineers after the old station was inundated by slack water from the construction of Bonneville Dam. Long since removed from the timetable, the crack passenger train is following the south bank of the Columbia through territory that once saw Northern Pacific trains running over the rails of the **OR&N.**

U. S. Senator Maurine Neuberger

THE NORTH COAST LIMITED inaugurated in 1900, was a transportation marvel in its day with impeccable service and elegant furnishings. It was the first train to the Northwest to feature such luxuries as electric lights, a library, barbershop and bathtub.

Northern Pacific Railway

Three Bridges and Tunnel, on Green River, Washington.

POWERED BY A 2-6-0 Mogul type, an NP freight train stands in the yard at Duluth, Minnesota, with its crew, in January 1893.

Northern Pacific Railway

NEAR NORTH YAKIMA, WASHINGTON in 1912 an eastbound passenger train, possibly the North Coast Limited, judging by the order of the head end equipment, hit the caboose of an eastbound freight. The almost new Q-3 class Pacific (Baldwin 1909) reduced the "buggy" to a pile of splintered lumber, and little remains of the caboose except the top of the cupola, behind the two men in white shirts. The air brake was still something of a novelty in 1912 and the words "AIR BRAKE" were prominnently painted on the sides of some boxcars.

Collection of Ed Noan

ONE OF NORTHERN PACIFIC RAILWAY'S crack transcontinental flyers stops at the Livingston, Montana depot. Note the spotless locomotive, doubtless the pampered pet of its crew. This is a Haynes photo made on October 7, 1895.

Northern Pacific Railway

ARCH ERECTED by the Chicago St. Paul Minneapolis & Omaha Rwy., in St. Paul to celebrate the opening of the Northern Pacific in 1883. Building in background is old NP headquarters at Broadway & 4th Streets. Arch is on 4th St.

Northern Pacific Railway

Chapter II

The Cascades and Stampede Tunnel

The decision to expedite construction of a line from the Columbia River, through Central Washington (primarily following the valley of the Yakima River), and across the Cascades to gain direct access to Puget Sound and the Northern Pacific terminal at Tacoma, was made during the administration of President Robert Harris, who had succeeded Henry Villard in January, 1884. President Villard had never really pressed for the completion of a mainline or "branch" across the Cascades to Tacoma, even though this was the intention of the original incorporators of the Northern Pacific. Villard preferred instead, the more circuitous route following the south bank of the Columbia River from Wallula to Portland, and then to Goble, Oregon where the Columbia was crossed by car ferry to Kalama, Washington, then north again by way of the valley of the Cowlitz and the Nisqually to Tacoma. This longer route to Tacoma used the rails of the Oregon Railway & Navigation Company, organized in 1879 by Villard. The Oregon Railway & Navigation Company line ran for a distance of 214 miles from Wallula, where the Walla Walla River joined the Columbia. The Northern Pacific was thus complete regarding service to the Pacific Coast, but was not complete in the sense that it operated over its own rails from Lake Superior to Puget Sound.

The original intention of the Northern Pacific to cross the Cascades directly to Puget Sound was subverted in favor of the Columbia River line, not entirely because Villard preferred the more southerly route and controlled the transportation on the Columbia River, but for other economic reasons as well. In the 1870's, Portland and the Willamette Valley, with a population of around 100,000 people, was the largest center of commerce in the Northwest, while Tacoma and Seattle, on Puget Sound, were just beginning to grow from towns of 4,000 and 7,000 population, and were regarded as more or less an extension of Portland's commerce. A main line that connected Portland directly with the East, and that also reached up into Puget Sound country to tap this growing area made good business sense.

There was also the greater cost of pushing a line across the Cascades where surveys had disclosed only two passes, both involving a rise and fall of between four and six thousand feet, with the additional expense and time necessary to build a summit tunnel. The Wallula to Portland line was a nearly water level grade down the Columbia, and even considering the heavy rock work involved (particularly in the 45 miles between the Dalles and Bonneville in the narrow gorge of the Columbia), the total cost was less. Chief Engineer Roberts, pointing out also the heavy snowfall and pack certain to handicap railroad operations in the Cascades, recommended, in 1872, that the Northern Pacific

THE WEST PORTAL of Stampede Tunnel, during its construction in the late 1880's resembled the burrowing of a giant mole. The contract for construction of the tunnel held by the Bennett brothers, carried a penalty clause if construction exceeded 28 months. They completed the tunnel slightly ahead of time, but construction was hampered not only by soft and fractured rock deep inside the mountain but by the height of the mountain over the tunnel that made it impossible to sink a central shaft down to the tunnel level so that more working facings could be utilized. All material going in, and all "spoil" coming out, had to pass through the same opening.

The large wooden building in the left foreground housed the first electric generating plant in the Cascades and provided power for the electric lighting system in the tunnel. Directly over the tunnel the trees have been cleared away so that survey crews could accurately plot the path of the tunnel and check on the alignment of the bore as work progressed.

Collection of Ed Nolan

first build the line down the Columbia, and later a "branch" eastward from Puget Sound.

There were further financial complications. In the early 1880's the Northern Pacific was having considerable difficulty raising construction money to complete the main line, and by utilizing the rails of the OR&N from Wallula to Portland, the NP was not faced with the heavy expenditures in building its own line along the north bank of the Columbia, a duplicate line which would have created a disastrous rate war between the NP and the OR&N.

The decision to proceed with construction of the

NELSON BENNETT

Cascade line (first called the "Cascade branch"), running from Tacoma to Pasco, and connecting with the main line going east, was precipitated by a number of events, not all necessarily of equal importance, but in the aggregate, extremely important to the Northern Pacific. The commerce of the Puget Sound region was growing rapidly, with increasing trade to the Orient, British Columbia and Alaska through the fine deep water ports of Seattle and Tacoma. Some of the finest timber in the United States stretched in huge forests right up to the summit of the Cascades, and lumber was being produced in the largest sawmills in the country. Coal was being mined, in quantity, in the Wilkeson, Carbondale and Newcastle coal fields. An expanding fishing industry, and a rapidly growing farming and dairying community added to the prosperity of the area.

There was also the matter of pacifying the citizens of Seattle, if possible, who were still miffed at the Northern Pacific for selecting Tacoma (30 miles away) as the western terminus of the road. Seattle, the larger of the two towns, regarded itself as the better port, and therefore, the most logical choice for a terminus. Although the Northern Pacific could live with the pique of the Seattle citizenry, it could ill af-

ford to have the Seattle citizens build a railroad of their own to the East, as they started to in July, 1873. The Seattle and Walla Walla was incorporated to run a line via Pasco over the same pass route in the Cascades previously surveyed by the NP. Fortunately, for the NP, the Seattle and Walla Walla fizzled out in 1875, at Argo, only three and one half miles from Seattle. Nevertheless, it must have caused some chills in NP headquarters at Brainerd, for the land grant in the Territories amounted to 40 sections to the mile, and the 248 mile long "Cascade branch" through virgin timber and rich farm land represented 6,920 sections of land with a potential value of millions.

The demand was growing also for a railroad to serve the Yakima Valley, which was proving a rich and fertile area for growing fruit and other crops.

Finally, continued dependence on use of OR&N rails along the south bank of the Columbia to Portland, to gain access to the Pacific Division of the NP (from Portland to Tacoma), involved the risk that the "harmonious interests" (Villard and his backers guiding both the OR&N and the NP through the Oregon and Transcontinental Company) could collapse at any time, leaving the Northern Pacific with a 214 mile gap in its rails between Wallula and Portland, and no east-west main line in either Washington or Oregon. In fact, President Villard resigned in 1884 when his

THE NP ENGINEERS' CAMP, located high in the Cascades, close to Stampede Tunnel, was the permanent headquarters of the engineering staff during the construction of Stampede Tunnel 1886-1888. The buildings were built of logs obtained from trees cut down right at the very doorstep of the buildings. The wood for heating and cooking was stored in a large lean-to type of structure attached to the main building, and rough outbuildings served as storage areas for supplies.

Northern Pacific Railway

73

complicated financial holdings collapsed, and in 1887 the OR&N was leased to the Union Pacific. Today it operates under the shield of that road, having been reorganized in 1910 as the Oregon Washington Railroad & Navigation Company, a subsidiary of the Union Pacific.

Under President Harris' administration, work began to move rapidly up the Yakima Valley. No particular difficulties were encountered on the long stretch from Pasco to Thrall (just east of Ellensburg), but on the west side, through the spectacular Green River Gorge, construction was slowed as the railroad became a series of bridges, cuts and fills, crossing and recrossing the Green River, as it climbed a steady grade towards the precipitous peaks of the Cascades.

The earliest surveys had determined that a permanent crossing of the Cascades could be accomplished only through a lengthy summit tunnel, and Mr. V. G. Bogue, principal engineer for the Northern Pacific, was given the task of locating a suitable pass, further to the south than the one discovered by D. C. Linsley, 11 years before, at the headwaters of the Wenatchee River. Extensive exploration resulted in the discovery of Garfield Pass, located some 75 miles east of Tacoma, at an elevation of 2,852 feet, on March 19, 1881.

The name Garfield Pass was short lived. Two survey parties put in the field by Bogue, deserted after being consolidated under an overly severe trail fore-man, and a member of the next crew to arrive nicknamed their site "Stampede Camp." The new name caught the fancy of the entire crew, and spread along the railroad so that Garfield Pass soon became known as Stampede Pass.

Bogue's assistant, J. L. Kingsbury, made the first location for the 1.8 mile long summit tunnel in August 1882, and four subsequent locations were made before W. H. Kennedy made the final location. All used the same exit point on the west side, but each designated different entrys on the east side. In 1885, President Harris inspected the final location, on horseback, approved the site, and the job was declared open for bids.

Among the bidders for the tunnel job at Philadelphia, in 1886, were Sidney and Nelson Bennett, two brothers, who had built the railroad from Pasco to Ellensburg some time before, using Mormon graders as part of the labor force. The Bennetts had established a reputation for getting things done. They had even borrowed money to make the payroll and keep the graders at work when NP funds had run short, knowing, of course, that when times were better they would be paid back by the railroad. The Bennett brothers won the contract to build Stampede Tunnel because of their low bid of $837,250. This amounted to only $85.00 per foot, and with the cost of timbering the tunnel, reached a total of $1,200,000. Other contractors thought the Bennetts had taken leave of

ENGINEERS OF A SURVEYING AND LOCATING PARTY during the building of the temporary switchbacks across the summit of the Cascades in 1886, before completion of Stampede Tunnel, pose in front of their camp.

Northern Pacific Railway

BORING STAMPEDE TUNNEL through the Cascade range in 1887 and 1888, gave the Northern Pacific a direct mainline between Puget Sound and Lake Superior, as provided in its charter.

Northern Pacific Railway

their senses with such a low bid. "Hadn't the Hoosac Tunnel, twice as long as Stampede Tunnel cost $13,-000,000?" Not only was their bid low, half of some of the other bids, but they also accepted a completion deadline of 28 months, and a penalty clause of $100,-000 if they failed to meet it. The Northern Pacific wanted to get through the Cascades as soon as possible, and the Bennetts had the job.

In February of 1886, Sid Bennett left Yakima with men and equipment transported on wagons,

sledges and mules to begin work on the approaches to Stampede Tunnel. At this time NP tracks were just beyond Yakima on the east, and Eagle Gorge on the west. Even though tracks were hastily pushed almost to Ellensburg, the tunnel location was still 50 miles away in heavy forest on the east side, and an additional nine miles to the site of the west portal, over the tops of the mountains.

On February 13, 1886, hand picked drillers began attacking the rock at the east portal with hand

75

DR. MORRISON is shown with his family standing directly in front of the small window of the Stampede Tunnel Hospital, located near the tunnel about where Martin is today. During the building of Stampede Tunnel many injuries and some fatalities occurred, and a hospital was constructed to care for the injured with Dr. Morrison in charge.

Northern Pacific Railway

drills, while another crew of men diverted a waterfall splashing ice water on them from 200 feet up the side of the mountain. Other crews erected barracks, a hospital, supply buildings and the engineers' headquarters. Using only hand tools and blasting powder, drilling in the tunnel was measured at the average rate of three and one half feet per day. The danger, the discomforts, the hard work, and the long cold winter days and nights caused the men to quit in droves. Superintendent Sid Bennett, wrote to his brother that he kept three teams busy, "one coming, one drilling and one quitting." After four months of agonizingly slow work, Nelson purchased a complete battery of Ingersoll air operated drills in Tacoma and put them into service. Production almost immediately doubled, and Nelson followed this up by building the first electric lighting plant in the Cascades to provide illumination in the tunnel. With power drills and adequate lighting, production increased so rapidly that shattered rock and spoil in the tunnel became a problem. Nelson solved this by building a "go-devil" traveling platform that ran on rails in the tunnel, so that after each blast, the platform came up level with the heading, and cars could be loaded underneath to carry away rock from both the bench and the heading. With this equipment in use, production jumped to a combined rate (east and west headings) of 14 feet per day by May of 1887.

While the tunnel was being built, the NP was bypassing the route with a temporary switchback system that ran around the tops of the mountains near the tunnel. There were three switchbacks on the east side and two on the west side of the summit to gain the altitude necessary to reach the great double horseshoe across the summit itself. Roughly eight miles of track was necessary to go slightly over two miles, since the switchbacks started and ended very near the east and west portals of the 1.8 mile long Stampede Tunnel. The grades encountered on the switchbacks were almost beyond belief—on one stretch a grade of 5.6 percent was encountered.

Much of the track laying had been done during the winter of 1886/1887, when the Northern Pacific, hurrying almost to the point of desperation to complete the Cascade line, employed thousands of Chinese to shovel snow off the raw grade. Right on their heels came the tracklayers and their equipment. Then came the spring of 1887, when the long frozen earth thawed, and the roadbed heaved and settled, developing soft spots. Fill dirt slid and was washed away by the melting snow. Track sagged, buckled and heaved along with the roadbed. Practically the whole length of the switchbacks had to be rebuilt to repair the damage. The building of the switchbacks was a notable engineering achievement, but fortunately for the Northern Pacific, they only had to operate it for a year, because nothing resembling a heavy tonnage main line operation could be carried on across the terrible grades.

There was a train limit of five cars, regardless of whether the train was freight or passenger. One 2-10-0 type (specially built for this service by Baldwin in 1886) was placed at the head end of the train, while another 2-10-0, running in reverse, was coupled to the back of the train. The 2-10-0's were equipped with special water brakes, while the rest of the equipment was fitted with the usual air and hand brakes. A brakeman was assigned to every two cars to tie down the hand brakes, while riding the tops of the cars across the switchbacks, and the rest of the crew was specially trained for this service. Scheduled time across the switchbacks was an hour and fifteen minutes—if all went well. The train would get underway, and by sawing back and forth across the switchbacks,

with the engines alternately pulling and shoving, the train would climb up one side and down the other. Going up grade was bad enough, but coming down again was the real hair raiser. Even a momentary loss of control could result in a runaway and disaster. Yet in spite of the extremely dangerous grade, the railroad never had a fatality on the switchbacks.

The completion of the temporary switchback in June, 1887 took some of the pressure off completing the line to Tacoma via the tunnel, but the Bennetts spurred their men on to meet the deadline, and avoid the penalties in the contract. On May 3, 1888, a blast opened a tiny hole between the east and west headings. By May 27, timbering had been completed, and the first train rolled through the tunnel. Crowds in Tacoma, Yakima and Seattle celebrated, dancing in the streets, for the NP was now a direct railroad from Lake Superior to Puget Sound.

THIS CLOSE-UP VIEW of a rotary plow crew was made near the east approach to Stampede Tunnel in 1887. The conductor stands on the blade housing of the rotary, with his derby hat, dark suit coat and heavy brass watch chain, all symbols of office and authority on the railroad.

Northern Pacific Railway

A SNOW BUCKING OUTFIT crosses Mosquito Creek Bridge in 1887 with rotary plows on each end and four locomotives between. Without the second plow facing in the opposite direction, a slide coming down behind the train could stall the entire outfit if the snow ahead could not be penetrated, or if the rotary blades were damaged by debris in a slide. Even with the added precaution of the second plow and several locomotives for power, rotaries were often stuck up on the switchbacks for long hours or even days as snow accumulated faster than it could be plowed away.

Northern Pacific Railway

Within three years after the completion of the Northern Pacific across the Cascades, the Northwest Territories had gained sufficient population, much of it due to immigration via the railroad, to become States of the Union. North and South Dakota became States on November 2, 1889. Six days later, on November 8, 1889, Montana became a State, followed by Washington on November 11, 1889, and finally Idaho on July 3, 1890. From Northeast to Northwest, along the Canadian border, the Union was complete.

A TREMENDOUS WOODEN BRIDGE, one of many built in the Cascades during the 1880's, is shown in this artist's drawing. Steel construction was a luxury to the Northern Pacific during this period, struggling as it was to complete 2,000 miles of railroad, and nearly every bridge—with few exceptions—was built of timber that was close at hand and free for the taking.

Collection of Jim Frederickson

A TRACKLAYING CREW in 1886 pose with their equipment on Mosquito Creek Bridge on the switchback route across the Cascades. The grade climbed at an incredible 5.6% in places on the switchbacks, and the snow packed 20 feet deep during the winter months. Even with all the inherent operational hazards, many crews regretted the abandonment of the switchbacks upon completion of Stampede Tunnel in 1888, for the tracks in this area passed through some of the most beautiful alpine scenery in all of North America. *Northern Pacific Railway*

LITTLE RECOGNIZED by many historians is the role played by thousands of Chinese in the building of the Northern Pacific Railway. As early as the 1850's large numbers of Chinese were in the Northwest mining gold that had been passed over or ignored by white miners. Others were operating laundries, gambling houses and assorted businesses in Ellensburg, Portland and Seattle. During the building of the NP across the Cascades in 1886/1888, working for less money than white men, they were employed by the hundreds shoveling snow so tracks could be laid on the switchbacks. Their attempts to improve their wages and working conditions were to little avail. After the completion of the road, they drifted away and helped to form the large Chinese communities that exist today in Portland, Seattle and Vancouver, B. C.

Northern Pacific Railway

Chinamen Shovelling Snow for Tracklaying near Summit of Swit

SHOWN IN THIS 1887 photo, is the summit of the switchbacks used by the NP to cross the Cascade mountains during construction of Stampede Tunnel.

Northern Pacific Railway

THE ARTIST'S CONCEPTION of the switchbacks across the Cascades, drawn in 1888, is correct in that five distinct levels were used to cross the summit, three on the east side and two on the west side. The nearly unbelievable grade of 5.6% in places called for the heaviest locomotives built up to that time, and a pair of 2-10-0's built by Baldwin in 1886 were used exclusively on the switchbanks.

Collection of Jim Frederickson

A CUT OF WORK TRAIN EQUIPMENT and boxcars are pushed back into one of the switchbacks during the winter of 1887. The switchbacks were completed in June of 1887 and operated for only one year—until May 1888—when Stampede Tunnel was completed. The winter of 1887 and 1888 was severe, and the temporary expedient of the switchbacks gave the operating department headaches it didn't forget for years. Slides, stalled trains, runaway equipment and accidents plugged the mainline time and again, and hundreds of men were called from as far away as Tacoma and Yakima to help unsnarl the tangles.

Northern Pacific Railway

DOWNGRADE FROM STAMPEDE TUNNEL, along the west slope of the Cascades, flows the Green River, a snow fed mountain stream. Usually a clear green in the deep quiet pools, it is churned to frothy white as it tumbles between rocky cliffs and over hidden rock formations. Some of the most spectacular scenery on the west side of the Cascades is here in the Green River Gorge. For a distance of about 30 miles, the railroad crosses and recrosses the river as it follows the watercourse from the west portal of Stampede Tunnel to Kanaskat, and along its banks a construction crew pauses in 1885.

Northern Pacific Railway

CONSOLIDATION TYPE NO. 1214, built by American Locomotive Company in 1901, is shown with its crew at Lester, Washington in 1907. Lester, located some 14 miles below the west portal of Stampede Tunnel, at the foot of the 2.2% grade, was a helper terminal and a scene of continuous activity as helper engines were coupled ahead of and behind the caboose for the long grind up to Stampede Tunnel. The last helper (a pusher) was uncoupled on the fly at the entrance to the tunnel, while the helper ahead of the caboose continued on through the tunnel to be cut off at Martin. From the blacked out headlight to the dirty and gritty brass bell 1214 shows the cumulative effect of soot and cinders that has covered nearly every inch of the engine and tender. Only six years old, the hard service in the Cascades has obliterated every trace of paint or gloss except for the removable engine numbers on the side of the cab.

Collection of Ed Nolan

LEAKING STEAM FROM EVERY SEAM around the smokebox, a Consolidation type on the point of an eastbound freight, posed for a picture in 1911 after emerging from Stampede Tunnel. Wisps of smoke, still visible in the tunnel entrance, and rising straight in the air indicate a calm day. Enginemen dreaded calm weather because of the long time necessary to clear the tunnel of smoke and gas. Only a strong east wind could clear the tunnel quickly and remove the ever present danger of suffocation in the smoky and steaming hot bore.

Collection of Ed Nolan

THE ONLY TEN COUPLED ENGINES to ever operate on the Northern Pacific were a pair of 2-10-0's, ordered by the railroad from Baldwin Locomotive Works and delivered in 1886 for service on the switchbacks. Numbers 1 and 2 (shown in 1904 at Ellensburg) were fitted with 46″ drivers, carried a boiler pressure of 150 lbs., and weighed 282,300 lbs. in working order—complete with tender. Unfortunately these two Decapods spent a good deal of their time in the shops and were a source of continuous trouble. The Northern Pacific learned a great deal from these engines and never repeated an order for more ten coupled types.

Collection of Ed Nolan

WESTON, bypassed in 1913 due to track relocation, was once an important communications link through Stampede Pass. Here in 1912, wives of the operators at Weston pose for their picture standing on the roof of the coal shed, and nearby, on top of the station roof, rests the primitive fire fighting equipment, the water barrel.

Collection of Jim Frederickson

JUST BEHIND THE CAMERA POSITION in this 1913 photograph, Weston is being bypassed by a new steel trestle that will carry the relocated mainline high above the heavy curvature of the old mainline.

Collection of Jim Frederickson

LOCATED at the foot of the sharp 2.2% westbound grade to Martin and Stampede Tunnel, Easton, Washington, was a beehive of activity during the days of steam. Easton was not only a helper station for westbound trains, but like its counterpart Lester on the west side, a layover point for crews, especially during the winter months. Overwhelmed by the seasonal rush of business, private facilities in this small mountain town were inadequate, and the NP built a hotel exclusively for the use of the railroad crews.

Collection of Jim Frederickson

DATA CLASS Z NOS. 3000-3015

Built—1907
Baldwin Locomotive Works

CYLINDERS
Diameter, H. P.	21½ ″
Diameter, L. P.	33″
Stroke	32″

WHEELS
Driving, Diam.	55″
Eng. Truck, Diam.	30″
Trailing Truck, Diam.	30″

BOILER
Diameter	84″
Pressure	200 Lbs.

FIREBOX
Length	117″
Width	96″
Grate Area, Square Feet	78

TUBES
Number	437
Diameter	2¼″
Length	21'-0″

Tractive Power, Lbs., 67,500
Factor of Adhesion,   4.68

HEATING SURFACE, SQUARE FEET
Tubes	5383
Firebox	225
Total	5608

CLEARANCE DIMENSIONS
Height, Rail to Top of Stack	16'-0½ ″
Height, Rail to Top of Cab	15'-2¼ ″
Width over Pilot Beam	10'-5 ″
Width over Runboards	10'-4 ″
Width over Cab	10'-3 ″

Valve Gear—Walschaert

WEIGHTS, WORKING ORDER
Drivers, Front, Engine	164,200 Lbs.
Drivers, Back, Engine	151,900 Lbs.
Engine Truck	18,700 Lbs.
Trailing Truck	20,200 Lbs.
Total, Engine	355,000 Lbs.
Tender	152,700 Lbs.
Total, Engine and Tender	507,700 Lbs.

WEIGHTS, EMPTY
Total, Engine	321,500 Lbs.
Tender	60,000 Lbs.
Total, Engine and Tender	381,500 Lbs.

TENDER, CLASS 17E
Capacity, Water	8,000 Gals.
Capacity, Coal	26,000 Lbs.

WHEEL BASE
Driving	30'-0 ″
Engine	44'-10″
Engine and Tender	72'-3 ″

BUILT BY BALDWIN in 1907, Class Z Mallet compound 3005, a 2-6-6-2 type complete with Belpaire firebox, was a duplicate of the early class L Great Northern engines, (also Baldwin built), the first Mallets to see service in the Cascades. Slight detail differences in the cab, headlight and tender are the only visible changes between the GN and NP versions. This particular locomotive was photographed near Lester in 1915 when it was in helper service between Lester and Easton.

Collection of Ed Nelson

"THEY CALLED IT STAMPEDE HELL!" This remarkable photo of the smoke conditions encountered by engine crews passing through the long tunnel was taken by Jim Frederickson at Martin, outside the east portal of Stampede Tunnel.

Prior to 1912, the 2 mile long Stampede Tunnel was the most dreaded bore on the entire railroad. The smoke, gas and fumes encountered by the crews was almost beyond human endurance, and a slow moving drag could fill the tunnel with fumes in a matter of minutes. In later years crews were provided with gas masks, and a ventilation system was installed after a fatal suffocation in 1912.

Much of the difficulty with Stampede was that it was arched near the center, and grades were encountered regardless of train movement, east or west. The arch acted as a natural trap for the rising smoke and fumes from the engine stacks and to further complicate matters, the roof of the tunnel leaked, making the roadbed soft and dangerous. Derailments in the tunnel were frequent, and unless the engines could be cut off quickly and moved outside the portals, the tunnel became a gas chamber. Little wonder train crews judged the success of a trip between Auburn and Ellensburg by the conditions they encountered in "Stampede Hell".

Collection of Jim Frederickson

WHEN THE SWITCHBACK ROUTE across Stampede Pass was abandoned in 1888, a dirt road was built that followed the old railroad grade. At the summit this elevation marker may be found today, while nearby, rotting timbers and rusting spikes are all that remain of the old railroad route.

Jim Frederickson

SURROUNDED by burned and logged timber the isolated little railroad town of Lester, Washington bustled with activity in the first half of the 20th century when steam was still the dominant power on the railroads. Today, as the diesels howl by on their way upgrade, or pass with a whine of dynamic braking, Lester, still isolated during the winter months and accessible only by railroad or snowmobile from Snoqualmie Pass, is only a shell of its former self.

Colletion of Ed Nolan

THE SIX STALL BRICK ROUNDHOUSE at Lester was a busy place in the days of steam with "hill power" continually coming and going. Six Consolidation types (2-8-0's), their smokebox fronts polished for the photographer have all been lined up facing out of the roundhouse, the reverse of their normal servicing position.

Collection of Ed Nolan

AN ASHCAT (fireman) assigned to a 2-8-0 waits with the engineer to begin another run up the mountain from Lester. The big scoop he is holding will seem even bigger by the time the tunnel is reached—14 back breaking miles up the 2.2% grade. In this era—1911—the 2-8 0's and early Mikado's like 1504 were fired by one man, but later the bigger classes of Mike's drew 2 firemen, as the increased firing rate was too much for one man without the assistance of a power stoker.

Collection of Ed Nolan

BLASTING OUT OF LESTER, a road engine and pusher boosts the eastbound North Coast Limited up Stampede Pass in 1912. This striking photograph of mountain operation on the Tacoma Division was made from the huge coaling dock alongside the mainline.

Collection of Ed Nolan

CIRCA 1916, the Lester milk-man pauses during his daily rounds with his pushcart and canine helper by the station at Lester to pose with a railroad employee in a camera study of times long since gone.

Collection of Ed Nolan

BAKING BREAD for emigrant section workers and other rail-road employees was done in these earth and rock ovens at Hot Springs, Washington, just west of Lester. The equipment is somewhat primitive, but one look at the huge loaves on the clean plank to the left would convince anyone of the culinary skill of the baker!

Collection of Ed Nolan

LITTLE CHANGED since it was built before the turn of the century, the station at Lester, a small mountain town, reposes in silence between trains.

Jim Frederickson

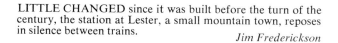

89

DURING THE "BIG SNOW OF 1916," Easton, Washington was buried in snow, and operations came to a complete halt on the mainline across the Cascades. Every type of snowplow the railroad owned was called into service, and extra track gangs and engine crews succeeded in temporarily restoring service in some areas only to have it halted again by more snow. Service was finally restored when the weather cleared, but for days the trains ran through deep cuts of snow from Easton west.

Collection of Ed Nolan

A ROTARY PLOW working the mainline at Easton breaks through a white trackless waste after the "big snow" of February 1916. The memory of that record fall still serves to mark time for the residents of Easton who experienced it.

Collection of Ed Nolan

CONDUCTOR HOUGH, from Auburn, Washington, sits on the stack of Pacific 2184 at Stampede in 1916. The engine had been stalled by deep snow, was struck by a slide that derailed the tender, and then further imprisoned by more falling snow. Note that the snow had managed to get inside of the headlight—probably through a broken engine number indicator.

Collection of Ed Nolan

PACIFIC 2184, on the head end of train #42, is locked in the snow at Stampede Pass under the tunnel telltale. To further complicate the situation, the tender is derailed and laying askew across the mainline. Evidence of the battering the passenger equipment has taken is shown by the plug of snow inside the broken window of the coach in the foreground.

Collection of Ed Nolan

MARTIN WAS THE NERVE CENTER for traffic through Stampede Tunnel prior to the CTC installation in 1958. At that time facilities were removed from Martin and all tunnel traffic remotely controlled from Easton. These photographs of the operators' quarters, section house, and station were taken during World War II by Jim Frederickson, then assigned to Martin as the 2nd trick operator (4 to midnight). Now an NP dispatcher in Tacoma, he developed his interest and skill as a railroad photographer on the Tacoma Division during World War II, and since has covered a large share of the Northern Pacific with his camera.

Jim Frederickson

Z-3 4018 IN HELPER SERVICE at Martin during World War II. The slogging Z-3's used as road engines and helpers in freight service were unsuitable usually as helpers in passenger service due to their 30/35 mph speed restriction, but were used occasionally when the passenger road engine would similiarly restrict its speed to the limit imposed on the Z-3's. Exceeding their speed restriction would result in both damaged rail and machinery on the old compounds.

Jim Frederickson

A ROTARY AND SPREADER are at work near Martin, in this winter scene, taken during World War II. Carrying the makers of this plow outfit is one of the unusual bay window cabooses that enjoyed a spell of popularity on the NP and SP&S. First used in mainline service, the bay window cabooses were relegated to branch and work train duty after proving to be highly unpopular with crews who were accustomed to the generous and high mounted cupolas of regularly assigned cabooses.

Jim Frederickson

A JORDAN SPREADER clears the track in Stampede Pass after a late winter snowstorm. When the snow was deep the spreader was coupled immediately behind the engine, with a rotary plow leading and worked in conjunction with the plow crew, but at other times, as pictured here, it was utilized separately.

Collection of J. E. Caron

NEAR MARTIN, WASHINGTON, in Stampede Pass, a rotary works to clear the tracks during a brief spell of good weather. Snow on the west slope and across the summit of the Cascades is a problem during the winter months. Then the moist ocean air, flowing in from the west dumps prodigious quantities of snow on the mainline. Rotary crews continuously on the move during the frequent storms, in the days before the sixteen hour federal law, often spent as high as 24 to 36 hours in the cab.

Jim Frederickson

AN EASTBOUND PASSENGER TRAIN with a Pacific on the head end, and one of the first diesels delivered to the NP, FT No. 6001 running as helper, pulls to a stop in Easton where the diesel will be cut off. Behind the long train the snow covered ramparts of the Cascades loom up under a gray winter sky, while in Easton, the sun is shining. On this day in the late 1940's, all the trademarks of a small railroad town of several decades ago are clearly in evidence: the high and stained water tank, the bell capped water plug beside the mainline, and the complexity of tracks leading to the ash pit and servicing facilities. *Jim Frederickson*

HAVING REFUELED AT THE COALING DOCK in the background, Challenger 5116 is spotted over the ash pits at Easton, having its ash pans dumped and fire cleaned before returning to Yakima. On the mainline, behind four FT units, an eastbound freight idles while the crew picks up orders. *Jim Frederickson*

AFTER COMING IN from Tacoma behind a four unit diesel, an eastbound freight prepares to leave Easton for Pasco behind a massive Challenger. The big multiple unit "growlers," in the early days of diesel operation, did not run straight through as they do today, but were used across the toughest parts of divisions. Then the trains were turned over to the less powerful, but more numerous steamers.

Jim Frederickson

TRAIN NO. 26, the North Coast Limited, slips down the east side of Stampede Pass just beyond Martin, Washington. Here the dual main and long siding ease the concentration of traffic using the single track through tunnels 3 and 4.

Jim Frederickson

CTC SIGNALLING has replaced the old upper quadrant semaphores at Martin for controlling traffic through the single tracked Stampede Tunnel and its multiple track approaches on the east and west. At night, the gleaming aspects, shining high above the rails, and the softly lighted trackside buildings, create an atmosphere of early day railroading that even the modern diesels and their strident air horns cannot dispel.

Jim Frederickson

BEFORE INSTALLATION OF THE CTC system on the single track between Stampede and Martin, through Stampede Tunnel and tunnel #4, occupancy of the single track was controlled by an interlocked Staff Block System that allowed only one train at a time—from either direction—to enter the block. The operators at Stampede and Martin had one staff between them that was passed to the engineer of the locomotive or units controlling the air as a train entered the block. Upon leaving the block the staff was passed back to the operator at the far end of the block and this operator assumed control of the Staff Block System. Further, the interlocked switches could not be aligned for movement through the area unless the staff was put through the staff machine in the office at either Stampede or Martin. Here, in a photo by Jim Frederickson, the engineer of an extra freight catches the staff as it is hooped up to him by the operator at Stampede.

THE WEST PORTAL OF TUNNEL 4 appears as a black hole in the mountain in this photo taken just beyond Stampede Station in the 1950's. The single track through tunnels 3 and 4 required a complicated interlocked signal system and the use of a "staff" passed to crews from the small elevated platform in front of the station. Only when the staff had been passed to the operator at Martin, at the east end of tunnel 3, and put through the staff machine in the station office, could the signals and switches be cleared for a conflicting movement.

Jim Frederickson

EASTBOUND NORTH COAST LIMITED emerges from the snowshed around the east portal of Stampede Tunnel in the winter of 1962. The waterfall in the background, tumbling 200 feet down the mountainside, had been diverted from its original course by dams and breastworks to permit construction of the tunnel to commence on February 13, 1886.

Jim Frederickson

EMERGING FROM STAMPEDE TUNNEL, the four "Covered Wagons" and Geep pull an eastbound freight that originated in the NP yards at Auburn, Washington. The long continuous 1% ascending grade stiffens to 2.2% from Lester to Stampede. This long, grinding climb has not overstrained the units, but the cab firewall behind the engineer and fireman has become hot enough to heat the entire cab, without necessitating the use of the cab heaters, on this cold March day.

Jim Frederickson

FT FREIGHTER HOWLS out of a snowshed around the east portal of tunnel 4 into the bright sunlight of a spring day.

Jim Frederickson

THE STEEP CUT on the eastward track leading into tunnel No. 2 on Stampede Pass caused many problems for the operating department. It was inevitably plugged, during times of heavy snowfall with drifting snow, and the steep sides of the cut were too high for the rotary to throw snow into the clear. The result was all too often, as shown here, a snowplow outfit stuck in the drifts, and derailed equipment. In this instance the plow and engine are being dug out by hand while the derailed caboose waits for sturdier assistance.

Jim Frederickson

THE SUPERINTENDENT'S "HI-RAIL" INSPECTION CAR, a Jeep Station Wagon fitted with extendable flanged wheels for service on the railroad, pauses at Eagle Gorge station on the west side of Stampede Pass in the late 1950's. Off the railroad the flanged wheels were pulled up and the car could proceed in conventional manner. The heavy springing, necessitated by the weight of the extra wheels and axles, made the car extremely rough riding on the highway and the railroad route was much preferred by those who had occasion to ride in the Jeep.

Jim Frederickson

EASTERN SLOPES of Cascade Mountains, near the Stampede Tunnel.

AN EASTBOUND TIME FREIGHT emerges from the snowshed at the east portal of tunnel 4. The diesel units, heeling to the super elevation, will soon pass out of sight around the far curve, and only a mile or so upgrade will enter the west portal of Stampede Tunnel.

Jim Frederickson

WESTERN Portal of Stampede Tunnel.

NOT FAR FROM AUBURN, WASHINGTON, along the lower reaches of the Green River, the hustling diesels of the westbound North Coast Limited drum across the deck of a steel bridge as the early morning sun reflects off the sides of the units.

Jim Frederickson

PREDECESSOR of the retractable wheel Jeep station wagon was a Ford sedan, number B-67, equipped with special flanged wheels mounted inside the regular wheels that enabled it to travel on rails. Not as versatile as the Jeep, it was nevertheless used on the Tacoma Division for years, and was equipped with special sanders and brushes to sweep the railheads clear in times of inclement weather.

Jim Frederickson

LOOKING LIKE THE FILLING IN A STEEL SANDWICH, a wooden caboose between two compound Z-3 class pushers, is ready for a jolting ride up to the summit of Stampede Pass. A sudden stop by lead pusher 4014 could catch the caboose in a nutcracker squeeze that would promptly reduce it to a pile of splinters. In the days of steam, this dual pusher operation, known as "one in and one on," was repeated day after day as the drags assaulted the mountain fortress of the Cacades from Lester and Easton.   *Jim Frederickson*

VIEW on Green River, Washington.

STEPPING LIGHTLY through the rain washed countryside, ten wheeler 1372 rocks and sways slightly along the Woodinville, Washington branch line en route to Redmond. The class S-4, 4-6-0, a 1902 graduate of Baldwin Locomotive Works, was one of 39 similar engines assigned to branch line way freight duties. Long a favorite of rail fans and model builders, the classic S-4's survived almost to the end of steam operation. Light on their feet, easy on the track, and simple to fire and maintain, they were ideal power for branch line and switching service.

Casey Adams

104

Chapter III

Steam Motive Power of the Northern Pacific

THE NORTHERN PACIFIC RAILROAD, the first of the Northwest transcontinentals, until the general acceptance of diesels after World War II, remained a railroad of steam power. The railroad cast its fortunes with steam, notably from Baldwin and Alco, after the turn of the century, and unlike the Milwaukee Road and Great Northern, resisted the temptation to electrify its tough mountain divisions. This reliance of the Northern Pacific on steam power (mostly coal burning except on the Seattle to Portland line where oil burners were used due to a lack of coaling facilities at Portland) was largely a matter of economics.

The Northern Pacific owned one of the largest coal strip mines in the country at Rosebud, Montana. This huge facility could deliver soft brown coal (lignite) for about 70¢ per ton, and the better quality coal from the railroad controlled mine at Roslyn, Washington could be delivered for slightly more. With plentiful supplies of fuel at hand, far cheaper than its competitors could buy, the railroad designed its power to take advantage of the cheap fuel. Lignite, to be utilized properly, requires grates of enormous size, and Northern Pacific modern power carried the largest grates ever to be applied to steam locomotives. The Northerns used grates of 115 sq. ft., the Challengers 152 sq. ft. and the monstrous Yellowstones, grates of 182 sq. ft.

With the exception of a pair of 2-10-0's, built for service across the Cascade switchbacks, the locomotive roster of the Northern Pacific up to the turn of the century, was relatively undistinguished with motive power characterized by 4-4-0's, 2-6-0's and a succession of Consolidation 2-8-0 types. Some 4-8-0's were placed on the roster, no doubt due to their success on the neighboring Great Northern, but it was the appearance of the Mikado 2-8-2 type that marked the beginning of a distinguished motive power roster that utilized some of the finest steam types in the United States.

The NP purchased the first class W, 2-8-2 type, in 1904 from American Locomotive Company. These locomotives, the first of the really heavy duty Mikados built in the United States, made the popular 2-8-0 (Consolidation) obsolete in the same type of service. The larger firebox on the 2-8-2, located behind the rear drivers, produced steam in sufficient quantities to give continuous power output at even high demand rates. The 2-8-2 required little maintenance, and was exceptionally stable around the vertical, horizontal and lateral axis, providing excellent riding qualities.

Orders were placed with American Locomotive until the NP had over 300 Mikes in service in six subclasses, starting with the inside bearing trailing truck classes W, W-1, and W-2, built between 1904 and 1910. The largest number of Mikes, the 125 engines of the W-3 class, were built between

NORTHERN TYPE NO. 2661 class A-3 was one of eight locomotives delivered by Baldwin in 1938, and the second series of Baldwin built Northerns to be fitted with 77″ drivers instead of the 73″ drivers of the class A's and A-1. The NP, having found a suitable compromise between the 73″ drivers of the earliest types and the 80″ drivers being applied to Northerns built for some other roads, would settle on 77″ drivers for succeeding orders. The 77″ Baldwin disc design wheel was remarkably strong and simple to balance. New improved methods were being developed to adequately cross balance the running gear to minimize dynamic augment at high speeds, with the result that the A-3 class locomotives were easy riding and stable even in the high 70's and 80's. The tractive effort of the A-3 was 69,800 lbs. as compared to 65,700 lbs. for the earlier A's, with the increased tractive effort largely due to both an increased boiler pressure (from 240 lbs. to 260 lbs.) and an increase in locomotive weight from 426,000 lbs. to 491,800 lbs.

Jack Anderson

1913 and 1920. Following the W-3's were 6 Mikes in the W-4 class (oddly numbered in the 2500 series) rebuilt from obsolete Prairie types—an experiment that wasn't repeated. The 25 locomotives in the W-5 class, built in 1923, were the only non-articulated engines on the road to carry their pumps on the front of the smokebox with the headlight centered under-

neath the pumps, departing from the usual NP practice of mounting the large headlight high on the smokebox and making them resemble a Great Northern engine.

Arrayed around this centerpiece of Mikados in the 1920s were a sprinkling of class Y Consolidations, some 70 class T Prairies (making the NP the biggest

26″ x 40″ and 26″ x 30″ cylinders that, from the front view, gave them something of a Norfolk & Western compound look. Not particularly large when compared to the 2-8-8-2's of some other roads (the engines alone weighed only around 480,000 lbs.), they rolled on small 57″ drivers and developed a tractive effort of 89,500 lbs. The Z-3's were used as road engines and helpers on both main line and branches on the Tacoma Division, in Stampede Pass, and further east in the Rockies and Bitterroots. They could be found on Evaro Hill west of Missoula, on Homestake Pass across the Continental Divide, going up Bozeman Mountain out of Livingston, and in Mullan Pass between Helena and Garrison. Their service on the Wallace, Idaho branch crossing Lookout Pass high in the rugged Bitterroots was memorable. This steep and sharply curving branch out of St. Regis, Montana with one of the stiffest ruling grades in the country—4%—reduced the pulling power of the Z-3's to a mere 600 tons.

In 1923, the NP purchased its last four 2-8-8-2 compounds from American Locomotive Company designating them class Z-4. Weighing 541,000 lbs., they were heavier and more powerful than the Z-3's and exerted a tractive effort of 107,300 lbs. The driver size remained at 57″, but the cylinder size was changed to 25″ x 39″ and 25″ x 32″. In common with the Z-3's, they were slow footed, and lacked the capability of moving a train at speed. Running light both were restricted to 30 mph., and to 35 mph. while pulling a train. These speed restrictions made the compounds, except for switchers, the slowest engines on the road. Even the elderly Prairies, Mikes and Consolidations could rattle off a solid 45 to 50 mph.

In service on the main line the compound Mallets were nearly as slow footed going downhill as they were going uphill and any attempt to push the speed above 35 mph. resulted in excessive maintenance, as the pounding and vibration set up by the small 57″ drivers shook the frames and machinery unmercifully. Track too took a heavy pounding from the drivers, and more than one track gang was kept busy straightening kinks and abused rail after a Z-3 or Z-4 exceeded its speed limit. Nevertheless, operated within their inherent limitations, they were serviceable engines capable of moving heavy tonnage, and many of the venerable compounds, surviving more modern engines, were utilized—particularly in the Cascades—right up to the end of the steam era in the late 1950's.

In addition the Northern Pacific had some older compound Mallets in service, classes Z, Z-1 and Z-2 built by Baldwin between 1907 and 1910, that were essentially duplicates, even to the Belpaire fireboxes, of the Great Northern class L engines that pioneered

user of this type in the country), dual service class S and P ten wheelers, some ancient class B American types dating back to 1887 and used on the lightest branch lines, class D Moguls built in 1888/1889, and a few class X 4-8-0's built in 1897.

For switchers the NP relied heavily on the 0-6-0 type, most of them built between 1901 and 1910 by both American and Baldwin. The most numerous were the 70 or so of the L-9 class built between 1906 and 1910. The heaviest and most modern switchers on the road were two classes of 0-8-0's, USRA types built in 1919 and 1920 by American.

By the mid 1920's the articulated locomotive roster included 21 class Z-3 2-8-8-2 Mallet compounds (American Locomotive 1913 and 1920) built with

AMERICAN TYPE 4-4-0 NO. 764, with its tender, stands directly in front of some most unusual trackwork in the NP yards at Seattle in 1901. No explanation has been offered for the switches without point rails, and it would seem to be no place to make switching moves at night. Horns decorate the huge oil burning headlight, and the folded back headlight cover was closed when meeting opposing trains at night to prevent blinding the other crew.

Collection of Ed Nolan

compound operation in the Cascades. These little 2-6-6-2's, numbered in the 3000, 3100 and 4000 series, were rated at around 60,000 lbs. of tractive effort—about equal to a W-3 Mike which was rated at 63,400 lbs. The elderly Mallets, fast approaching the end of their service life because of excessive maintenance costs and slow speed when used in main line service, were being replaced by the faster Mikes. The Mikes were easier on the track, could handle about the same tonnage, and were virtually maintenance free by comparison. The few old Z's remaining until the late 1930's, were relegated to the slowest of drag and work train service.

Passenger service on the Northern Pacific between the turn of the century and the late 1920's, was almost completely dominated by a large fleet of 4-6-2 Pacific types arranged in six subclasses. The lanky little 69″ drivered Baldwin built Q's and Q-1's of 1903 and 1904 weighed 205,000 lbs. and had a tractive effort of around 31,000 lbs. The modern Alco built Q-5's and Q-6's, of 1920 and 1923, rolling on 73″ drivers, were nearly as large and heavy as a USRA 4-6-2, with an engine weight of around 320,000 lbs. and a tractive effort of 44,000 lbs.

Between the early Q's and the modern Q-5's and Q-6's were two other classes of Pacifics, the Q-3's and Q-4's, built by Baldwin in 1909 and 1910. Rolling on 69″ drivers and basically similar to the Q's and Q-1's, they were slightly heavier with an engine weight of around 240,000 lbs., and carried a boiler pressure of from 180 to 200 lbs. Out of over 200 4-6-2's ranging the system in the late 1920's, 123 were still in service as late as 1945.

Strangely, the NP, like the neighboring Milwaukee Road, completely ignored the 4-8-2 Mountain type that found such favor on the Great Northern wheeling heavy passenger and mail trains. The Mountain type was nearly 30% more powerful than the Pacific, and as the name implied, far better suited for service in the mountainous terrain that the NP encountered in Montana, Idaho and Washington.

As passenger trains were becoming increasingly longer and heavier, and schedules were becoming more demanding, even the modern Q-5 and Q-6 engines were being worked at full capacity on the level districts and required helpers in the mountains. While it was possible to build a bigger and heavier class of Pacific for passenger service, to do so would require revisions in the existing track and bridge structures to accommodate the increased axle loadings. The firebox size also was limited by the ability of the two wheel trailing truck to carry the increased load. It was clearly evident that something bigger and better than the existing 4-6-2's was necessary, but this newer and bigger locomotive would have to take into account the load carrying limitations of track and structures.

In 1926 the Northern Pacific took the biggest stride in motive power development in its history

when it received the first 4-8-4 or Northern type of locomotive (so named by the publicity department of the railroad) built in the United States. These big engines, numbered from 2600 through 2611, products of American Locomotive Company, and designated class A by the railroad, were half again as powerful as the most modern Q-6 Pacific type. Weighing 426,000 lbs. (with tender 739,000 lbs.), rolling on 73″ drivers, and carrying a huge firebox over the four wheeled trailing truck to effectively burn the soft and fast burning lignite, they developed a tractive effort of 65,700 lbs. With the trailing truck booster cut in, they developed 75,000 lbs. of tractive effort, but the booster proved to be more of a maintenance complication than it was worth, and was eliminated in later series of engines.

Long boilered, fitted with large roomy cabs and trailing huge rectangular tenders, the big Northerns could reel off the long miles across the prairies and along the Yellowstone River between St. Paul and Livingston without apparent effort, as the heavy Pullmans swayed along behind their massive tanks. In mountainous country, the big engines could battle their way up the 2% grades and screech their way

A FAVORITE WITH ENGINE CREWS and the motive power department on the Northern Pacific were the high stepping, thoroughly modern Challengers. The crews liked their easy riding qualities and the higher rate of pay that went along with a Challenger assignment, while the management liked the speed capabilities and high horsepower at speed which contributed to keeping a fast schedule. Here Z-8 No. 5137 booms down the high iron near Yakima, Washington with an eastbound trainload of freshly iced reefers filled with fruit from the orchards of Central Washington.

Jim Frederickson

around 12 degree curves so sharp that the front sanders at times sprayed the roadbed rather than the railhead, with the big drivers slipping, catching and then slipping again until the curve had been rounded, while the big stack was racketing the exhaust off the surrounding rock cliffs or up out of the cuts. With the ability to work full out in the 70's and 80's, while pulling a 1,000 ton load, and without pounding the rail to the shape of wet spaghetti, the 2600's were justifiably the pride of the motive power department. Not only was the NP impressed with its new power, that could also double in fast freight service and literally run the wheels off of a merchandise drag, but other railroads were impressed too, for variations of the new Northern type were soon running in the East, Midwest, Southwest and across the Canadian border.

The success of the class A design was evidenced by the eventual purchase by the NP of five different subclasses of Northerns totaling 49 engines. Following the purchase of the original A's in 1926, the NP purchased the famous all roller bearinged Timken engine "1111" or "Four Aces" that became, with slight modifications, No. 2626 on the NP, and the only engine in the A-1 class. In 1934 and 1938, the A-2 and A-3 classes, the first of the 77" drivered NP Northerns, were delivered. The NP had learned from the experiences of other roads operating in the Rockies, that an 80" wheel was fine out on the prairies and along the river grades, but up on the mountain grades, squealing around tight power robbing curves, the 77" wheel was a better compromise. In common with the earlier engines, the A-2's and A-3's were fitted with conventional cabs, but trailed the new "water bottom" tenders rather than rectangular tanks mounted on separate frames. The A-2 locomotives were distinguished by the odd appearing "box pox" style drivers that were never reordered for subsequent models. Instead, the Baldwin disc driver became standard on all later models. The A-3 class served as the prototype for the SP&S 700 class, and was identical to it except that the SP&S burned oil and had different lettering and numbering.

The culmination of the Northern type was reached in 1941 and 1943 with the purchase from Baldwin of 18 locomotives of the A-4 and A-5 class. These locomotives were identical except for the substitution of some allocated material such as chrome steel and light alloys that increased the weight by 7,000 lbs. The total weight of the A-5's (including tender) was a staggering 952,000 lbs. making them the heaviest Northerns ever built with the exception of the Santa Fe's wartime 2900 class that was about 2,000 lbs. heavier. With an overall length of 112' 10" and a height of 16' 4¼", carrying a boiler pressure of 260 lbs., fitted with 28" x 31" cylinders, and rolling on 77" disc drivers, the big 4-8-4's were rated at over 5,000 horsepower with a tractive effort of 69,800 lbs., and were just as versatile in fast freight service as they were in pulling the varnish.

Riding the chafing plate of the A-4's and A-5's was the huge all welded centipede tank of 4-10-0 wheel arrangement that was finding increasing favor

IN SPOKANE in March of 1951, 4-8-4 No. 2604, carrying green flags as the first section of train #2, the North Coast Limited, leaves for the East with 15 sleepers of troops from Fort Lewis. Challenger No. 5115 had brought the heavy train into Spokane.

Dr. Philip R. Hastings

CONSOLIDATION 1274 CLASS Y-2 rolls grandly through the Green River Valley between Auburn and Kent, Washington with a trainload of logs bound for the sawmills along Puget Sound. The little 2-8-0 is a 1902 graduate of Alco, and was among the last of the type purchased by the Northern Pacific. Although weighing a bare 100 tons they were not as heavy as either an 0-8-0 or one of the Prairie types, they were good branch line power and served the Northern Pacific right up to the end of the steam era in the late 1950s. The Y-2's were unique in that they were fitted with 63″ drivers and were quite fast for a freight engine. The other 2-8-0's, however, classes F-1, Y, Y-1 and Y-3 were all low wheeled with 54″ drivers standard. This resulted in a tractive effort of around 42,000 lbs. as compared with the 39,000 lbs. of the Y-2's.

Jim Frederickson

MIKES 1797 AND 1804, north and south bound on extra freights, pass on the multiple track along Commencement Bay in Tacoma. Exceptionally good looking freight power, the W-3's were characterized by centered headlights, compact cast steel pilots, big cabs, side mounted pumps, and cab roofs with a large tapered overhang that covered the narrow gangway. The tenders were typically NP — exposed channel underframe, four wheeled trucks, large doghouse and an oil compartment that reached nearly to the back of the short tank, while mounted on the left side was a huge back-up light salvaged from scrapped engines.

on roads in the West that had big power with big appetites for fuel and water. The fourteen wheels, not only spread the weight of the huge tank better than did the conventional six wheel trucks, but the guiding action of the lead truck and the lateral play built into the pedestal mounted axles, made the tender more stable and better riding at speed on tangent track.

The A-4's and A-5's combined the modern appearance of welded tenders, disc drivers, and vestibule all weather cabs with the traditional graphited smokeboxes, side mounted pumps, and brass bell hung out over the NP styled headlight. This blending of the old and the new in the locomotives' design, resulted in an engine that remained unchanged, except for the addition of lighted number boards, from the day it rolled out Baldwin's Eddystone plant until the final days of steam.

In 1928, the NP had purchased from Alco the largest locomotive that would ever operate on the NP rails—the 2-8-8-4 simple articulated type No. 5000 class Z-5. Put into service between Mandan, North

112

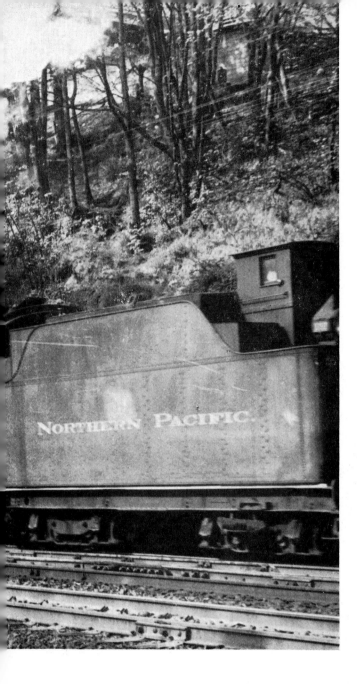

limited the engines to maximum speeds of 30-35 mph., restricted firebox and ashpan capacity necessitating frequent ashpan cleaning stops, poorly balanced machinery that made the locomotive hard on the track, and a general inability to cope with fast freight requirements. The net result was a heavy investment in what were essentially pusher and helper engines, confined to helper districts—a costly utilization practice.

The first four Challengers class Z-6 delivered by Alco in 1936, were fitted with 69″ drivers, 23″ x 32″ cylinders, carried a boiler pressure of 250 lbs., and exerted a tractive effort of 104,500 lbs. Complete with tender they weighed 1,039,600 lbs. A second group of eight engines were delivered late in the year, followed by nine more in 1937 for a total of 21. The Z-6 possessed a quality lacking in the older Mallets, the ability to roll freight at speed. Well balanced, easy riding and possessing huge fireboxes to keep up the steam at high demand rates, they could get down and pull at a steady 12 to 15 mph on heavy grades, and once over the top of a grade or rolling along the low gradients along the river routes, they could move tonnage at a steady 50 to 60 mph.

In 1941 and 1943, six Z-7's and twenty Z-8's were delivered. Basically these engines were the same as the earlier Z-6's, but the driver size was increased to 70″, the boiler pressure was raised to 260 lbs., the weight was increased to 1,081,000 lbs. and the tractive effort was increased to 106,900 lbs. Like the late model Northerns, the Z-7's and Z-8's were equipped with centipede tanks and very large all weather vestibule cabs.

In appearance the Challengers were quite different from any articulated locomotives in service on the NP. The large disc drivers have an appearance of speed even while the locomotive was standing still. The steam and sand domes, spaced along the length of the boiler, rather than being concentrated at the back, gave a more balanced symetrical look, while the small high pressure cylinders under the huge boiler, and compact massive "bandstand" just under the smokebox mounted pumps spelled power and flexibility.

The shadow of the diesel fell across steam operations on the NP, as it had on other roads throughout the U. S., for two and four cylinder steam engines were simply no match for 16 cylinder diesels and electric traction motors that could be multiplied to form any horsepower locomotive desired. Main line steam operations continued well into the 1950's, but as more and more diesel locomotives were received, by the road, scrapping of steam power reached wholesale proportions, until by late 1958, steam power was non existant.

Dakota and Glendive, Montana, the monstrous "Yellowstone" replaced two heavy Mikes, and cut in half the train miles between these two terminals. Eleven more of the 2-8-8-4's were ordered from Baldwin and delivered in 1930. The twelve locomotives were modernized during World War II and with new welded frames and roller bearings continued in service well into the 1950's until replaced by diesels.

In 1936 the NP made a radical departure from the low wheeled slogging type of articulated locomotive and ordered the first Challenger 4-6-6-4 type to appear in the Northwest. The NP, for some time, had been aware of the limitations of the 2-8-8-2 type: poor riding qualities, lack of stability at speed that

CLASS W 2-8-2 NO. 1612 pulls into Arlington, Washington with the Darrington local loaded with fir wood chips and logs. Darrington, which once billed itself as being in the "timber bowl" of the Northwest, is located along the Sauk River, about as far east in the North Cascades as one can get today by either car or railroad. Beyond this point the mountains form an impenetrable barrier to the eastern part of the state, making it necessary to either go south and then east through Stevens Pass, or north into British Columbia and then east via Hope and Princeton.

Jim Frederickson

ALONG THE COMPARATIVELY little known branch of the NP in Washington between Elma, on the line to Grays Harbor and the Pacific Ocean, and Bremerton, site of the sprawling U. S. Navy Shipyard, a local freight peddles along the light iron of the sub-division of the Tacoma division behind an inside bearinged trailering truck Mike. The line eventually terminates at Bangor, Washington on Hood Canal, site of a tremendous Navy ammunition depot.

Jim Frederickson

A PAIR OF CHALLENGERS doubleheading in Montana was not an uncommon sight, particularly as power was being balanced between terminals, but not as common was the sight of a Challenger cut in the train about a third of the way back. In the above photo a pair of Z-8 class Challengers are hustling a fruit special across the open prairie with twin columns of dark coal smoke to trace their path.

Jim Frederickson

BESIDE THE VALLEY of Hangman's Creek in Spokane, W-2 class 2-8-2 No. 1902 leads a local west on the NP main line. At Cheney, Washington, 25 miles south of Spokane, the local will leave the main line for Coulee City, near Grand Coulee Dam, deep in the heart of Central Washington.

Dr. Philip R. Hastings

THE NORTH COAST LIMITED, train #1, arrives in Missoula, Montana in June of 1941 behind an old wooden Pilot Pacific (built in 1904) after a very rare occurrence. Northern 2652 broke down and stand by power had to be called to pull the train in. Fortunately the high mounted, but 69″ drivered 4-6-2 only had to cope with level and descending grades to get #1 into Missoula, for even if two of them had been double headed the theoretical 62,000 lbs. of tractive effort still wouldn't have equalled the 69,-800 lbs. of the big class A-2 Northern.

W. R. McGee

A CHALLENGER SLOWLY DRIFTS up to the water plug as on old Z-3 type with large flat topped low pressure front cylinders finishes getting its drink in this meeting in Yakima Canyon.

Jim Frederickson

MALLET-COMPOUND Z-3 class, No. 4016, awaits assignment in Yakima, Washington. Built by Alco in 1917, the 57″ drivered 2-8-8-2 had a tractive effort of 89,500 lbs. Designed with the tough Cascade grades in mind the big engines of this class were slow but sure footed on the curving mountain grades. With long straight barreled boilers, large pilot decks and small tenders they resembled in some respects the GN 2-6-8-0's that were also used in the Cascades. While not handsome engines, they were interesting and served the NP well.

Casey Adams

AT SUNSET a doubleheaded freight prepares to leaves Yardley in Spokane as a brakeman "bends the iron" to the main line beside an old side door caboose. Once the upper quadrant semaphore clears, Mikes 1738 and 1816 will go to work with a vengeance, and the now lazily drifting sooty coal smoke will column into the sky as the exhaust rackets off nearby buildings and equipment.

Dr. Philip R. Hastings

MOST NUMEROUS of all NP switch engines were the little 0-6-0's of the L-9 class. Eight of them, including No. 1126 were oil burners, while the remaining 63 were coal burners. Fitted with 51″ drivers that were almost universally applied to steam switchers and rated at 31,000 lbs. of tractive effort, they were in service for a half century after rolling out of the erecting shops at Alco and Baldwin, between 1906 and 1910. 1126 demonstrates the flexibility of its side rods and running gear in this engine terminal scene as the 2nd and 3rd drivers rest in a depression while the lead driver is on level track.

Jim Frederickson

NP TEN WHEELER No. 1372, heading up an early morning "Casey Jones Special" fan trip, passes the interlocking tower outside the North Portal of the tunnel beneath downtown Seattle.

Fred Spurrell

IN THE YARDS AT HILLYARD, Washington, GN 4-8-4 No. 2550 is in the background, while 4-6-6-4 No. 904 waits on the ready track for westbound freight. Remarkably similar in appearance to a Union Pacific Challenger from this camera angle, the distinctive water bottom type tender, extensively used on NP and SP&S heavy power, is a dead giveaway to the ownership of the big Challenger.

Dr. Philip R. Hastings

MIKADO 1674 RUNNING AS HELPER TO 2626 on a special fan trip, roars through Auburn, Washington with bell ringing before swinging to the big curve through town and heading east toward Stampede Pass. The high stepping oil burner is running easily here on level and tangent track, but a few miles further, with the track swinging first one way and then the other as it rises above the foothills of the rugged Cascades, all 46,600 lbs. of tractive effort of the 2-8-2 will be called upon to help the big Northern.

Jim Frederickson

AGAINST A BACKDROP of mountains of the Bitterroot Range on the Montana-Idaho border—a range so steep and tortuous that surveyors of the Northern Pacific swung far to the north around Lake Coeur d'Alene to avoid meeting the range head on while laying out the profile of the main line—a Z-3 takes water at Borax, Idaho on the St. Regis to Wallace branch line. This branch line, serving the rich mines of Wallace, was one of the stamping grounds of the compound Z-3s, but even the brute force of the 2-8-8-2's was humbled by the curves and 4% grades. Any time the train weight exceeded 600 tons, it was necessary to double the hill, and even 600 tons was too much in inclement weather or if the engine was not up to full rated power.

Dr. Philip R. Hastings

CROSSING THE WIDEST PART of the Stillaguamish River just north of Arlington, Washington, Mikado 1612, class W, sets the heavy steel deck of the truss bridge to trembling as the 270,000 pounds of Brooks (Alco) built 2-8-2 comes through. The freight is working its way north through Arlington, Sedro Woolley, and Wickersham to the border at Sumas and an interchange with the Canadian Pacific.

Jim Frederickson

121

IN THE WHEAT COUNTRY of the Palouse, near Moscow, Idaho, fast freight 662 thunders along the branch line powered by a pair of ubiquitous W-3's. The most numerous of the Mikado subclasses on the railroad, 125 of these were built by Alco between 1913 and 1920. The W-3's, in company with the later built W-5's, represented the most powerful class of 2-8-2's. Rolling on 63″ drivers, they had a tractive effort of 63,460 lbs. while carrying a boiler pressure of 200 lbs. and an engine weight of 341,000 lbs. Their weight kept them off some of the branches due to bridge loading restrictions, and in these areas the older and lighter W, W-1 and W-2 classes held the assignments.

Dr. Philip R. Hastings

CHALLENGER 5136 on the turntable at Livingston, Montana.

Jim Frederickson

4016 APPEARS AGAIN, this time in branch logging service on the west side of the Cascades during 1946. The train is en route from the small town of Ravensdale, in the foothills of the Cascades, to the yards at Auburn.

Stanley H. Gray

NP NO. 4, THE "ALASKAN," moves around the "Big Curve" at milepost 187, along the Missouri River at Lombard, Montana. A named local out of St. Paul, the "Alaskan," long since removed from the timecard, heels to the curve in this shot by NP conductor W. R. McGee on July 28, 1947.

W. R. McGee

JUST A COUPLE of years away from extinction Northern No. 2653 stands on the main line near Billings Hardware Company in 1956. The handsome Northern with its dirty side rods and running gear, and the stained and weathered boiler, is a far cry from the gleaming flanks and polished steel of a few years before when it enjoyed its lofty status on the head end of main line passenger assignments. *Russell D. Porter*

JOINT NP/UP SERVICING FACILITIES at Lewiston, Idaho, stabled a variety of older power for use on the lightly constructed Camas Prairie. A UP 0-6-0 faces the camera while three Mikes, two UP's and one NP occupy the adjacent track. *Dr. Philip R. Hastings*

SP&S CHALLENGER NO. 900, a Northern Pacific Z-6 design, still sports its GN headlight, a holdover from the days when it was running for the Great Northern. Challengers 4000 and 4001, never popular with the GN, were sold to the SP&S, and on the shallow grades along the Columbia River, turned in magnificent performances on tonnage fast freights.

Dr. Philip R. Hastings

ON A RAINY winter morning in Tacoma, an NP freight slowly drifts by the order stand as the conductor hoops up an order.

Jim Frederickson

EXTRA 900 WEST crosses the Spokane River on the GN bridge and approaches Fort Wright Junction, where SP&S rails diverge to the south towards Pasco and Portland.

Dr. Philip R. Hastings

AT SOUTH BEND, Washington, the western end of the Aberdeen branch, not far from the Pacific Ocean, Mike 1621 turns its ancient combine on the wye.

Jim Frederickson

SP&S 4-8-4 NO. 702 passes a clear block and heads for the Hillyard engine terminal after coming in on train No. 4 from Portland.

Dr. Philip R. Hastings

WITH THE FIREMAN leaning far out of the cab window watching the backing Pullmans, Mike No. 1728 backs a troop train out of Union Station in Tacoma before heading up the hill in South Tacoma on its way to Fort Lewis.

Jim Frederickson

ON THE CAMAS PRAIRIE, a westbound log train from Headquarters drifts downgrade from Summit with UP 2-8-2 No. 2504 leading and No. 2711 behind.

Dr. Philip R. Hastings

THE FIREMAN OF Q-6 CLASS Pacific No. 2261 looks back from the high cab for a signal to highball. The big Pacific, most modern of the 4-6-2's on the NP roster, will make light work of the three car local.

Jim Frederickson

A LONG PARADE of empty boxcars destined for wheat loading farther along the Washington Central Branch are led past the old station at Medical Lake by Mikado No. 1904. The "C. W." branch diverges from the main line at Cheney, Washington some 16 miles southwest of Spokane and meanders from Cheney for 186 miles, covering the heart of Central Washington wheat country, eventually reaching the western terminus in the small yard at Connell.

FORMER Great Northern Challenger No. 4000, now SP&S No. 900, blasts a column of oil smoke skyward as it fights upgrade, westbound beyond Spokane, Washington, April 21, 1951.

Dr. Philip R. Hastings

TEN WHEELER NO. 1362 approaches the interlocking with the Union Pacific at Attalia, Washington not far from Pasco, on the Columbia River. Union Pacific outfit cars appear in the background and spotted along the siding to the left of the picture.

Jim Frederickson

SP&S ENGINE NO. 502, an elderly Mike of GN parentage, backs its work train off the spur at Marshall, Washington where it had been parked overnight.

Dr. Philip R. Hastings

EXTRA 4025 WEST tops the summit of Lookout Pass on the Wallace, Idaho branch, and with a few final resounding blasts from the stack, will shut down and drift into the small yard. The Wallace branch, with its 4% grade, reduced the power of the Alco built compounds to 600 tons in good weather, and around 80% of that in winter weather, when the grease in the car journals was stiff as old taffy.

Jim Frederickson

SHOP GOAT #9, resplendent in new paint, poses at the shops in South Tacoma. Rebuilt from a conventional 0-6-0 switcher, the little goat still shows its origin in the long and deeply arched roof and the patchwork appearance of the cab and end sill. It has been modified with water bunkers mounted beside the boiler.   *Jim Frederickson*

A "JACK OF ALL TRADES" on the Northern Pacific, the 2-8-2 Mikado, pulled down main line and branch service, with both freight and passenger assignments, ranging from Superior and Duluth on the far eastern end of the Northern Pacific line to tidewater in the far Northwest. Here, Mike 1795 pedals down the main line at Superior, Wisconsin with Duluth, Minnesota in the background.

Russell D. Porter

A PAIR OF MIKES, with the comparatively rare W-5, trailing an auxiliary water tender, followed by the other Mike, also trailing an auxiliary tender. Together they head up Extra 1838 West, two miles west of Billings, Montana in the fall of 1952.

W. R. McGee

Z-3 2-8-8-2 NO. 4020 CRESTS Lookout Pass in Montana and starts down the 4% grade eastbound, retainers having been set on all cars. The head brakeman, riding the tender, checks the train.

Dr. Philip R. Hastings

NP Z-3 NO. 4025 STARTS the climb over Lookout Pass on the Coeur d'Alene Branch. The short train is consistent with the Z-3 tonnage rating of 600 tons over the 4% grade.

Dr. Philip R. Hastings

DURING THE PRESIDENTIAL CAMPAIGN of 1952, Northern 2626 headed a one car special to Portland, Oregon to bring Vice-Presidential candidate Richard Nixon to Tacoma and Seattle. Due to a change in plans by Mr. Nixon, the special was never used, and is shown here, flying the white flags of an extra movement, returning to Tacoma.

Jim Frederickson

SPOKANE PORTLAND & SEATTLE Challengers Z-6 No. 900 and Z-8 No. 910 rest between freight runs at the GN engine terminal in Spokane.

Dr. Philip R. Hastings

WORKING HARD, two NP Mikes pull a northbound freight into Tacoma along the shore of Commencement Bay not far from Half Moon yard, while the head end brakeman prepares to "unload" from his perch by the dog house.

W. Wilkinson

THE NP Z-5 CLASS was almost as imposing at rest as it was in action. It was 120′ 6″ long, the length of three 40′ box cars and its 16′ 4″ height to the top of the stack was considerably higher than even the tallest boxcar. A hostler standing on top of the huge boiler filling the sand domes was fully two stories off the ground. Although they would not normally encounter anything tighter than a 12 degree curve in mainline service in the Rockies, the Z-5s were designed to squirm around curves as tight as 22 degrees in yards.

Curiously the prototype Z-5, No. 5000 or Yellowstone, named for the river the NP followed, was built in 1930 by Alco, long a builder of NP locomotives, while the following locomotives of the class, No. 5001 to No. 5011, were built by Baldwin. One explanation offered for this is that the NP regarded the locomotive's performance so highly, as a result of extensive testing in the "badlands" between Mandan, North Dakota, and Glendive, Montana, that they wanted fast delivery of the rest of the class and Alco, busy with other orders, was not able to do so.

The huge Yellowstones replaced in service between Mandan and Glendive 28 heavy Mikes that singly were restricted to 1,500 tons and doubleheaded something less than 3,000 tons. The Z-5s, going it alone, hauled 4,000 tons over the same district. In addition, they effectively speeded up the service, and saved fuel and the cost of another crew.

Although capable of running faster, the Z-5s were restricted to 35 miles per hour by employees' timetable instructions because the 63″ drivers didn't allow room for completely satisfactory counterbalancing at high speed and could pound rail unmercifully as well as the locomotive's frame and running gear.

The whopping 153,400 lbs. of tractive effort (with booster cut in) rated the Z-5's right along with the GN's R-2 class and such later day behemoths as the "Big Boy" and the Yellowstones used on the iron range by the D. M. & I. R. The pressure exerted on the conventional brass bearings by the 723,400 lb. weight of the locomotive was tremendous, and during World War II, the locomotives were modernized with roller bearings and new frames. Their solo performance has yet to be equalled in the diesel age, and nothing has appeared since on the NP to equal their 1,125,400 lbs. total weight.

Jim Frederickson

139

A MASSIVE CHALLENGER receives the attention of the shop forces in the Northern Pacific Shops in Livingston, Montana—the largest shops on the NP between the Pacific Coast and St. Paul. The heavy and classified repairs received by NP locomotives here served to keep the shops busy day and night.

Collection of Marv Hoskings

THE MASSIVE BRICK and stone passenger station in Livingston, Montana, some 1,000 miles west of St. Paul, also served as the division offices and the operating headquarters for the Yellowstone Division—the first of the mountain divisions.

Collection of Marv Hoskings

THE HIGH RAMPARTS of the Rocky Mountains loom in the background of this early 1940 photograph of the business district of Livingston, Montana. Just beyond the yard limits, the battle with the grades began and continued west over 1,000 miles to the Pacific Coast and tidewater.

Collection of Marv Hoskings

ALONG THE SHORE OF PUGET SOUND, just south of Tacoma, Mike No. 1784 with folded smoke deflector and ringing bell pulls a long string of Northern Pacific logging cars. The oil burning 2-8-2, a real work horse, reflects the pride the NP took in its motive power. Excepting for some staining around the smokebox and across the canvas covered cab roof, it is in nearly mint condition.

W. Wilkinson

P & L BRANCH PASSENGER TRAIN #312, behind Pacific No. 2222 runs beside Hangman's Creek as it nears Spokane. Shortly after this photo was taken in 1950, the schedule was discontinued. In the background, the tall supporting legs of the Union Pacific trestle trace their triangular shape against the surrounding hills.

Dr. Philip R. Hastings

AFTER PUSHING a freight to Reubens, helper engines UP 2-8-2 No. 2100 and NP 2-8-2 No. 1521 wait "in the hole" on the Grangeville Branch while returning to Lewiston, Idaho. Passenger train #312 with NP No. 1365 on the point passes on Arrow main line, bound for Spokane.

Dr. Philip R. Hastings

NP 4-6-0 NO. 1383 with Stites (Idaho) local freight has just switched the Evergreen Lumber Mill, and is now crossing the Clearwater River over a bridge built in the 1890's which limited engines to Class S-4, or lighter. Soon after this photo was taken in 1950 the bridge was replaced.

Dr. Philip R. Hastings

A WESTBOUND FREIGHT crosses over an elderly S curved trestle that spans Lapwai Creek in the depths of Lapwai Canyon. The train has just descended from the upper level in the background and a wheel cooling stop will soon be necessary.

Dr. Philip R. Hastings

ALONG THE MULTIPLE TRACK main through Tacoma a southbound extra freight works its way out of town behind a travel stained and hard working Mike. The battered gondolas behind the engine are typical of those used in log service. After a few years of hauling logs they are fit for little else as the rough service literally reduces them to bent skeleton frames.

W. Wilkinson

BEHIND PACIFIC No. 2194, the NP morning train to Port-land leaves King Street Station in Seattle, in the late 1930's. The GN's Empire Builder has pulled in just minutes before, and the 2500 class Mountain has pulled off and backed into the clear, while a switcher, coupled to the cars of the Builder, waits for the NP train to clear the switches before moving to Holgate Street passenger car yard.

Stuart Hertz

NORTHERN PACIFIC 4-8-4 No. 2626, the most famous Northern on the railroad, is posed for an official picture, at Seattle, just after its purchase by the road in 1933. The Timken trademark still decorates the ten-der and the cab and headlight have not, as yet, been altered to conform to NP practice.

Collection of Bill Converse

SP&S EASTBOUND "Western Star," train #4, slips downgrade behind 4-8-4 No. 700 at Marshall, Washington. The connecting train left Portland the night before and is due in Spokane the following morning to connect with the GN's Western Star—the renamed Oriental Limited.

Dr. Philip R. Hastings

MORNING CONNECTION to Tacoma for the westbound North Coast Limited waits at East Auburn behind Pacific No. 2216.

Jim Frederickson

ENGINE NO. 700, an NP A-3 design built for the SP&S, leads Spokane Portland & Seattle train #4 the "Oriental Limited," made up of both SP&S and GN equipment, across the GN trestle over the Spokane River for the GN connection in Spokane.

Dr. Philip R. Hastings

ON A QUIET SUNDAY A.M.
the postman has mail sacks
ready for southbound passenger
train #311 on the P&L Branch.
Pacific #2256 has just entered
the Branch from the main line.

Dr. Philip R. Hastings

CLASS W MIKADO NO. 1549, one of the first 2-8-2's ordered by the Northern Pacific between 1904 and 1907 smokes up the yard and considerable surrounding territory in Tacoma dramatically illustrating why some cities passed "anti-smoke ordinances" specifically aimed at the steam locomotive. When this picture was taken in the 1950's, the old 2-8-2 was nearly a half century old and showed the infirmities of old age—leaky flues, labored exhaust, clanking side rods and poor combustion. Still the venerable old battler had its day of glory as road diesel 5011 had broken down and 1549 had to be called to pull it and its train into town. The old hog rolled triumphantly into the yard with headlight gleaming and ancient rods marching off the miles while the new streamlined road diesel, silent and cold, followed behind.

W. Wilkinson

WITH THE VETERAN HOGGER watching for the signal ahead to clear, Challenger 5115 waits for Northern 2604 backing down to pick up the eastbound troop special that the Challenger has just brought in to Spokane. The terminal tracks ahead of No. 5115, due to the camera angle and foreshortening effect of the lens look as rough as those found on logging railroads, but negotiating rough trackage was of little concern to the flexible six coupled 4-6-6-4's that could, if need be, worm their way through tight curves that would put rigid framed types on the ground. In practice these big engines, because of their weight, were pretty much confined to main lines and the stouter trackage in terminals and yards.

Dr. Philip R. Hastings

WITH 1728 LEADING, a caboose for the crews trails behind a long parade of old Pullmans. Then follows Mike No. 1800 and a Baldwin yard switcher. Behind the last engine the 2% grade of South Tacoma hills falls away and around the curves. With a 170 ton locomotive almost at his back, a crew member in the cupola of the caboose leans back on the black leather cushions and watches the action and the scenery.

W. Wilkinson

W-3 NO. 1728 pulling a troop extra to Fort Lewis, Washington during the Korean War shouts up South Tacoma hill—where "mountain grade" operating rules are in effect—under a canopy of dirty gray oil smoke. The big Mike has lost its extended piston rods as evidenced by the patches on the front cylinder covers, and the solid grayish/ black colors of the locomotive is relieved only by the engine numbers and the road name lettering on the tank. Except for minor modifications the engine is basically unchanged since emerging from the Brooks Works erecting shop before World War I.

Out of sight, back around the curve, another Mike is working equally hard helping 1728 fight the uphill grade while behind the steam pusher a Baldwin yard switcher is digging in with its 1,000 hp. Unmistakable sign of the continuous battles with the grade, and the maximum tractive power needed to overcome it — where even a brief slipping of drivers means a stalled train—is the white powdered sand that covers the ties and base of the rails on the inside (up hill) main.

W. Wilkinson

A FEW MILES SOUTH of Spokane, Washington the mainlines of the Union Pacific, Milwaukee Road, the Spokane Portland & Seattle, and the Northern Pacific all converge at the little railroad town of Marshall, Washington. Marshall was one of the favorite spots of Dr. Philip R. Hastings (now of Waterloo, Iowa) for observing and photographing the activity of four of the Northwest's class I carriers. Unlike other remote spots passed by only one or two railroads, action here at Marshall was almost continuous, and on this August day in 1950, the famed Doctor has caught "Main" extra 2607 west moving upgrade past the NP tower controlling the P&L Branch junction and S. P. & S. connection.

A LITTLE CLASS L-9 switcher is working the industry spurs in Tacoma not far from Union Station whose dome is visible at the far left. This late spring day is warm and hazy, and the crew enjoys a momentary lull in the action.

W. Wilkinson

THIS MOST UNUSUAL picture of a firebox interior was taken by Jim Frederickson at Laurel, Montana while in the cab of Challenger No. 5141. The huge firebox, 20′6″ long, 9′6″ wide and about 7′ high was the largest ever applied to a 4-6-6-4 so that it could efficiently burn the lignite or "brown coal" used by the NP.

IN ST. PAUL NORTHERN 2666, class A-3, on the head end of the North Coast Limited, waits for the "highball" and departure to Minneapolis to begin the long race to Livingston, Montana, 1,008 miles to the west. At one time, this was the longest through run in the country, without changing power. As newer classes of Northerns arrived on the NP they were usually put into service between St. Paul and Livingston as this was the most demanding portion of the transcontinental schedule, and older Northerns then were put into service west of Livingston.

Jack Anderson

IN A MAGNIFICENT photograph of Northern Pacific steam operations by Jim Frederickson, W-3 class Mike No. 1800 crosses the 15th Street bridge in Tacoma.

SOUTH OF TACOMA, Washington, close by the waters of Puget Sound, 2601 hustles the noon train out of Seattle to Portland, Oregon. Two Southern Pacific cars are carrying the rear markers and at Portland will be cut into the SP overnight "Cascade" to San Francisco. During the fall and winter months this sea level line is often plagued with heavy fog that rolls in off the Sound reducing the visibility from the swaying cab to swirling mists that reflect the headlight beam right back at the engine. Under these conditions, the unprotected grade crossings are extremely hazardous and the usual joviality of the engine crew is cut short by the intense concentration on the roadbed ahead. The station platforms at Seattle and Portland, glowing with soft mist shrouded lights are welcomed by the headend crews as they mean that, except for the short return to the roundhouse, the trip is over.

Jim Frederickson

ON THE CAMAS PRAIRIE, NP Motor B-14, running as passenger train No. 343 from Grangeville to Lewiston, emerges from the horseshoe tunnel at the apex of Lapwai, Canyon, April 28, 1951.

Dr. Philip R. Hastings

155

WITH A CANOPY of white exhaust smoke laying back over the coaches and diner, Northern No. 2610, one of the A class engines built by Alco, streaks along the shore of Puget Sound south of Tacoma with a Seattle Times "Carrier Special."

Jim Frederickson

S-4 CLASS TEN WHEELER No. 1372 peddles across a little deck girder bridge near Redmond, Washington with a "Railfan Special" in 1958.

Casey Adams

UNDER THE WATCHFUL EYE of the operator at Woodinville, Washington, engine No. 684, the last remaining American type on the Northern Pacific, is eased back around the wye while being returned from a display in Bellingham, Washington. The little 4-4-0 was found on the Nez Perce & Idaho Railroad rusting away in the weeds. Repurchased by the NP it was carefully restored to mint condition by the Parkwater Shops in Spokane in 1951.

Jim Frederickson

OUT ON THE FRIGID PLAINS of North Dakota, 344 miles west of St. Paul, Timken engine No. 1111 steams softly at Jamestown on the head end of Northern Pacific No. 2, the eastbound North Coast Limited. Returning to St. Paul, after an extended trip west to demonstrate the efficiency of an all roller bearing equipped engine in NP service, the big Northern went on to become NP engine No. 2626, the only member of the A-1 class. From 2626 on, every NP 4-8-4 built was equipped with roller bearings.

Collection of Ed Nolan

SP&S 4-8-4 No. 701, a duplicate of the NP A-3 class Northerns, waits at the GN depot in Spokane for train #3, the westbound "Western Star." The 701 will depart at 9:45 P.M. with the Portland section over the SP&S.

Dr. Philip R. Hastings

ALONG THE YAKIMA RIVER, deep in the Yakima canyon in central Washington westbound No. 4010 has a meet with an eastbound drag and takes advantage of the delay to take water before continuing on to Ellensburg, Washington while the fireman cleans the fire (a continuous chore with poor coal) and uses a broom handle to poke at a clinker that is reluctant to break up and pass through the grates.

Jim Frederickson

SP&S EXTRA 537 East with local freight moves out onto the tremendous GN trestle across the Spokane River in this photograph taken in March 1951.

Dr. Philip R. Hastings

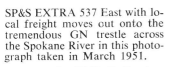

ON THE HEAD END of a northbound passenger train, engine No. 2601, the first class A Northern type delivered to the road in 1926, poses in Tacoma at Union Station. Clearly visible behind the rear drivers is the very large ash pan mounted directly on the trailing truck. Even more unusual is the fact that this engine—like others assigned to the Portland, Oregon run—is an oil burner, since Portland does not have coaling facilities.

Jim Frederickson

ALCO BUILT CLASS T, 2-6-2 Prairie type was photographed in Tacoma by Willard Wilkinson in the early 1950's. At one time there were over 150 of the class T and slightly heavier T-1's, all built in 1906 and 1907, on the NP roster. Having a tractive effort of around 33,000 lbs., they were somewhat more powerful than the little L-9 and L-10 class switchers and quite a bit more powerful than the numerous S-4 class ten wheelers. Fitted with 63″ drivers, carrying a 200 lb. boiler pressure, and weighing just over 100 tons they were well suited to a variety of duties, switching, transfer, local runs and main line. Many of the parts of the Prairies were interchangeable with those of the early W class Mikes and this served to prolong the life of both classes.

WITH A WESTBOUND work extra SP&S Mikado No. 551, obviously a GN design with Beleaire boiler and Vanderbilt tender stops for orders at Scribner, Washington.

Dr. Philip R. Hastings

FIVE DAYS BEFORE Christmas in 1936, Northern No. 2653 fights its way upgrade on Butte Mountain on the tough 2.2% at Welch about ten miles east of the Continental Divide—elevation 6,381'.

W. R. McGee

A BRAKEMAN on the back platform of an NP caboose peers cautiously around the end of the caboose at an approaching GN Alco "covered wagon" at McCarver street station in Tacoma.

Jim Frederickson

ON THE CAMAS PRAIRIE, a joint NP-UP operation, the morning passenger train from Riparia crosses the Clearwater River behind a Union Pacific 2-8-2 No. 2714.

Dr. Philip R. Hastings

EXTRA 1663 WEST, the C. W. Branch local freight, passes the junction of P&L Branch on the main line at Marshall, Washington.

Dr. Philip R. Hastings

THE AIR CONDITIONED engine terminal, at dusk, in Orofino, Idaho harbors UP 2-8-2 No. 2100, facing the turntable, and NP 2-8-2 No. 1527 parked next to the open sand house.

Dr. Philip R. Hastings

"THE FOUR DEUCES," Q-4 class Pacific, is about to leave the NP station in Spokane with train #311, the morning local to Lewiston, Idaho.

Dr. Philip R. Hastings

W-3 1748, RUNNING BACKWARDS for 40 miles on the rear of freight #662, helps the two Mikes up ahead to the summit of Clearwater Canyon at Howell, Idaho.

Dr. Philip R. Hastings

A PAIR OF VENERABLE MIKES, class W and W-2, push with a combined tractive effort of 96,000 lbs. against the drawbar of an equally venerable wooden (but steel underframed) caboose. The action is taking place in Tacoma, Washington, in the early 50's, on the stiff and curving 2% to South Tacoma and the old prairie line.

W. Wilkinson

HAVING JUST FINISHED COALING, Z-8 class Challenger No. 5138 displays its compact pilot deck, massive pump heavy smokebox and retractable coupler before heading out to the main line. The deeply arched cab roof is reminiscent of Union Pacific power, as is the centipede tender, but the distinctive headlight on the pilot deck—a modified pyle type—although smaller than most NP headlights, still clearly identifies the locomotive as an NP engine.

Jim Frederickson

0-6-0 1076, FRESHLY SERVICED and with steam pressure building, is being swung on the turntable before being spotted on the ready track for the second shift in the yards at Auburn. Contrary to the popular belief that steam engines were always dirty and decrepit in appearance, many roads, including all of those that served the Northwest, took great pride in the appearance of their locomotives and even their little yard goats. The running gear might be dirty and stained, and the smokebox gritty with soot, but the boiler, cab, domes and flanks of the tender reflected the road name and engine numbers with pride.

Jim Frederickson

HEADING FOR THE MINES and the 4% grade on the NP's Lookout Branch in the rugged Bitterroot mountains, class Z-3 No. 4025 dusts the Milwaukee Road's caternary over the joint use trackage not far from St. Regis, Montana. The huge barrel headlight on the pilot deck, the ash can size front cylinders, and shovel-like steel pilot all contribute to a look of plodding power—typical of older NP Mallets.

Jim Frederickson

ELDERLY CLASS W MIKADO No. 1592 is spotted near the modern steel coaling tower in Paradise, Montana. Steel coaling towers were rare on the Northern Pacific, although a similar, but larger, tower was also built at Livingston, Montana.

Jim Frederickson

CLASS Y-3 CONSOLIDATION 1207 had some embarrassing moments at Auburn, Washington in August, 1939. The hostler, thinking that the turntable was being lined for 1207, opened the throttle and proceeded to move forward as the turntable slowly swung in front of 1207. Actually, the turntable was being lined for another engine on the next track, and kept right on moving past as 1207 neatly did a toe dance right off the edge of the pit and buried the pilot and lead wheels in the soft dirt at the bottom of the pit. The big hook was called to return matters to normal.

R. L. Bennett

EXTRA 5136-5147 EAST, with 87 cars, thunders along the Yellowstone River in Montana, by the Springdale Bluffs on a magnificent day late in the fall of 1952. Challengers double heading was not a usual practice, but was employed when power was balanced between terminals.

W. R. McGee

ON LABOR DAY 1967, the "Casey Jones Special" from Seattle to Ellensburg was photographed a few miles from East Auburn, as the special was about to cross the Green River.

Jim Frederickson

A BUILDER'S PORTRAIT SHOWS an NP caboose built around the time of the first World War by Pacific Car & Foundry, Renton, Washington. The little wooden "buggy" with a steel underframe was extensively used on the western divisions of the NP, and for its size was very comfortable. The cupola in particular with upholstered leather seats, built almost like a couch, was a choice spot to ride, and the view from the tall windows was excellent. A few of this type of caboose are still in service on NP branches in 1968.

Collection of Bill Wardell

ALONG THE YAKIMA RIVER between Ellensburg and Yakima, Washington, an old compound Mallet, No. 4017, its huge slab side rods nearly touching the ballast with each revolution of the wheels, works its way west with 59 cars on May 5, 1941.

W. R. McGee

SP&S EXTRA 901 WEST has just emerged from tunnel 19, headed up the 1% grade out of the Spokane River Valley. Outbound engines are working hard upgrade so that the steamers cannot shut off through the quarter-mile of passageway beneath Spokane's Riverside Cemetery. Exhaust smoke trapped in the engine cab, while in the tunnel, drifts out of the engineer's window and pours out of the tunnel portal after the caboose emerges.

Dr. Philip R. Hastings

NO. 2608, CLASS A 4-8-4 TYPE, one of the first Northerns delivered to the NP in 1926-27, leads an eastbound "trooper" out of Tacoma during World War II. The big oil burner, along with others of the original class A series (2600-2611) was assigned to the Tacoma Division for service through and west of the Cascades because of tight clearances in Stampede Tunnel. Also, later engines from class A-1 No. 2626 were roller bearing equipped and were needed on the east end of the system, from St. Paul west, where higher speeds were reached and maintained for long distances.

Jim Frederickson

Z-5 5002, with safety pops lifting and steam trailing from the cylinder cocks on the rear engine, shakes the ground in Livingston, Montana as it pushes behind a mile long string of westbound high cars and tankers. Possessing the largest firebox and grates ever applied to a steam locomotive, to permit the efficient burning of lignite, the huge Z-5's when working hard, could dust a larger area of right of way with cinders than any other class of NP power.

Jim Frederickson

BETWEEN ASSIGNMENTS to Portland, Northern 2601 steams softly under the smokejack at the roundhouse in Seattle. Large number boards, and big flat lensed headlights with an odd triangular shaped number plate on top characterized the front ends of NP steam power. The centered headlight came into vogue on the NP after World War I. Older power usually featured headlights mounted high and off center on the smokebox front, giving an old fashioned look to the engine that even rebuildings and the addition of a new cast steel pilot couldn't help much.   *Mike McLaughlin*

EXTRA 5140 WEST beats its way upgrade near Marshall, Washington at sunrise in a display of smoke and steam.

Dr. Philip R. Hastings

ALCO BUILT class Y-1 2-8-0 switches the yard at Wallce, Idaho on a warm September day in 1950 when steam still ruled on the Wallace branchline. The elderly and low numbered little Consolidation is unique in appearance due to the visored headlight without the customary NP number board mounted above it. Except for the channeled underframe on the tank—a trademark of NP power—the little kettle could pass for a UP or SP engine.

Dr. Philip R. Hastings

MIKADOS 1516 AND 1735, with their heavy exhaust casting a pall of smoke over the landscape, pull freight #662 up out of the Clearwater River Canyon near Bovard, Idaho. Another W-3, 1748 is pushing hard at the rear, keeping the slack bunched, while it helps the train up out of the canyon.

Dr. Philip R. Hastings

THE MOST POWERFUL class of steam switchers were the 24 engines in the G-1 and G-2 classes, numbered 1170-1173 and 1174-1193 respectively. Built by Alco in 1919 and 1920 they were, with the exception of minor details, USRA designed locomotives. Solid, simple and efficient they developed 51,000 lbs. of tractive effort and were all hand fired coal burners.

Jack Anderson

W-3 1748 RUNS IN REVERSE as the rear pusher helps on freight #662, the "Highball." Two more Mikes on the head end are running in normal position as the train leaves Camas Prairie tracks (joint UP-NP operation) along the Clearwater River.

Dr. Philip R. Hastings

MIKE NO. 1506, in a flurry of exhaust, slips its drivers on the S shaped trestle over Lapwai Creek at is moves up-grade in Lapwai Creek Canyon with an eastbound freight on the Camas Prairie. The train will pass through a horse-shoe tunnel at the blind end of the canyon and double back on the upper track to reach the summit. NP W class Mikes were rated at only 500 tons on this grade.

Dr. Philip R. Hastings

IN THIS PHOTO taken at Spalding, Idaho in 1950, UP and NP Mikes, No.'s 2100 and 1521, wait for NP passenger train No. 312 to pass the junction of the First and Second Subdivisions of the Camas Prairie. The engines are en route back to Lewistown after helping a freight up Lapwai Creek Canyon on the Second Subdivision.

Dr. Philip R. Hastings

ON THE CAMAS PRAIRIE, a joint UP-NP operation, two MacArthur class engines (renamed from Mikado during World War II by the UP), 2504 ahead and 2711 behind, have lifted a log train over Summit from Headquarters and are drifting downgrade toward Orofino.

Dr. Philip R. Hastings

CROSSING PACIFIC AVENUE in Tacoma, Mikado 1706 powers a troop train up onto the 2% grade that leads to the old "Prairie Line," and south and east to the huge Army facility at Ft. Lewis.

Jim Frederickson

SPOKANE, PORTLAND & SEATTLE 2-8-2 553, a curious blend of NP & GN motive power design, drifts out of the sunset, with only the caboose left from a local freight run, as it approaches the GN main line at Fort Wright Junction.

Dr. Philip R. Hastings

ABOUT 2 MILES WEST of Taft, near the Montana-Idaho border, No. 4025 claws its way up the brutal 4% grades of Lookout Pass on its way to Wallace, Idaho. Constant curvature complicates the struggle as the boiler attempts to keep moving straight ahead while the front engine articulates to the curves and wheel flanges shriek and howl in protest against the outside rail. 4025 is running with an almost clear stack, but as the effect of the struggle upward begins to tell on boiler pressure, the stack will erupt in billowing clouds of smoke and the cinders will fall in a continuous shower.

W. R. McGee

A TALL SEMAPHORE BLADE indicates clear as A-5 No. 2681 roars around an upgrade curve west of Livingston high in the Rockies. The huge tank of the big Baldwin dwarfs the two cattle cars coupled behind it, while 70 some cars to the rear, a Yellowstone type (2-8-8-4) keeps the slack bunched as it adds its 145,000 lbs. of tractive effort to the pull of the Northern.

Jim Frederickson

WHEN REFERRING to the steam motive power of the Northern Pacific, too often the talk is in terms of the more glamorous power, the big engines such as the Northerns, the Challengers, the Yellowstones and the famous 2626 —the Timken engine No. 1111. However the 2-8-2's or Mikes were in reality the core of the motive power roster around which the other engines revolved, almost like satellites. The Mikes were found in every conceivable type of service from Duluth to St. Paul, to Livingston, Mandan, Spokane and Tacoma. Mikes pulled the troop trains, helped in heavy fast passenger service, powered the mainline freights, roamed the heavier branches, pulled diesels when they went dead, switched in some of the yards, and rode the turntables everywhere. As late as 1946, there were still 309 Mikes on the active roster. There were inside bearinged types like 1682, dozens of W-3s with the extended piston rods poking out of the front of the cylinders, and the occasional W-5's with pump heavy smoke box fronts that gave them something of a GN look. The NP was proud of their Mikes, and most of them were well maintained right up to the end of steam operations. Here a hostler checks the sand dome of 1682, Class W-1, a beautiful example of the workhorse of the NP roster.

Jim Frederickson

THE SECOND SECTION of the eastbound Mainstreeter, 2nd No. 2, climbs out of Hangman Creek into Spokane behind a Z-8 class Challenger. The first section, running just minutes ahead of this section, is the regular North Coast Limited, while this section is a solid troop special enroute east.

W. R. McGee

AMONGST THE HIGH PEAKS of the Rockies, west of Livingston, Montana, a mighty class Z-5 articulated shoulders into westbound tonnage, keeping the slack bunched, while far ahead a dual service Challenger type road engine leads the way through the ever deeper rock cuts and tightening curves as the summit is approached. The speed is a steady 12 to 14 miles per hour, and the semaphore blades of the block signals slowly fall to a horizontal position as the roaring 5003 passes.

Jim Frederickson

North Coast Limited with 18 cars, races along the broad curves following the Clarks Fork River near Belknap, Montana on June 15, 1941.

W. R. McGee

THIS PHOTO of engineer Walt Stevens and fireman A. C. Larson in the cab of engine 1693 was taken not long after the W-1 class Mike was built in 1910. Remnants of an early air operated firebox door mechanism are still visible in the primitive backhead. The doors were once automatically opened by an air cylinder actuated by a foot pedal, but because of the maintenance required, the company refitted the doors with a manual system.

Collection of Ed Nolan

TEN WHEELER 328, with a way freight in tow, drifts slowly over a grade crossing in Rush City, Minnesota. Part of an undelivered 1907 order for the South Manchurian Railways, this Alco built ten wheeler found a home on the Taylor Falls-Duluth branch of the Superior Division. Some 20 tons lighter than the 195,000 lb. S-4 class ten wheelers, the nine locomotives of the S-10 class possessed only 26,600 lbs. of tractive effort, little more than the venerable American types. Fitted with 57″ drivers, they were too slow for passenger service and spent most of their days on the lightly trafficked branches in mixed and way freight service. Top heavy, but light footed power, the S-10s could squirm through trackwork usually restricted to switchers, and for this reason, excelled in branchline way freight service.

Collection of J. W. Anderson

MAIN STREET ACTION at Coeur d' Alene, Idaho as ten wheeler 1355 leads a way freight through town.

Jim Frederickson

THIS UNUSUAL ENGINE, on the NP roster, was Heisler No. 4 used on the logging train around Yacolt, Washington just after the turn of the century.

W. R. Swanson

HEADED INTO MiNNEAPOLIS in 1952, 2-8-2 No. 1545 leads a way freight past a "prairie skyscraper"—one of the numerous wheat elevators in this flour capital of the world.

Russell D. Porter

THIS CLASS Z compound articulated was photographed in Montana, not long after the locomotive was delivered in 1907. Some of the 16 locomotives of this class survived into the 1930's, and as far as can be determined, the last one was scrapped in Tacoma in 1939.

Marvin Hosking

CLASS L-9 switcher derailed itself while backing over compacted snow and ice in Minneapolis November 1952. Faced with the cold and miserable job of re-railing the tender, the crew studies the situation before reaching for the re-railing frogs carried on the frame of the tank.

Russell D. Porter

THE LAST AND THE LARGEST compound articulateds purchased by the NP were the four locomotives of the Z-4 class (American 1923). The Z-4's were assigned to main line service in Montana, where No. 4500 was photographed at Butte in 1949. Good examples of slow slogging power, they were largely employed in drag service as the little 57" drivers simply were not capable of wheeling a freight at much more than 30 to 35 mph even under ideal conditions.

W. R. Swanson

W-3 MIKE, on test in Washington in 1917 carried 2 firemen to keep the steam up. Not equipped with stokers, when first delivered to the NP, the big 2-8-2's were more locomotive than one man could fire—particularly so when the engine was working hard and the poor quality soft coal was sucked right on through the firebox, across the grates, and out of the stack.

Warren Rehberg

BROMART, WASHINGTON, located about a mile south of the small yard at Snohomish on the branch at Sumas, had about the most condensed servicing facilities to be found anywhere on the NP. Here engines stopped to coal and water before tackling the hill into Snohomish. *Jim Frederickson*

A PRIME EXAMPLE of an NP class D-2 Mogul, Baldwin built in 1888, was photographed at the NP shops in St. Paul in 1935. The glossy gray boiler shows to advantage in this well lighted photo contrasting with the gloss black cab, domes, running gear and tank.

W. R. Swanson

NUMBER 2600 (1926) was the first modern, high capacity, high horsepower passenger locomotive that could double in fast freight service in mountainous terrain, could cope with western distances and western grades without sacrificing speed over the level districts, and possessed the capability to cross division after division with nothing more than routine servicing. The exploits of the big 2600's are well known on the long distance run between St. Paul and Livingston, but equally impressive was the performance of other 2600's assigned between Seattle and Missoula, a run not quite as long as the Livingston assignment, but far tougher from the standpoint of grades and keeping to the timecard.

Fred Spurrell

SNOW, STEAM AND STEEL are caught by Russ Porter as 1574 works its way into Minneapolis from Anoka on Thanksgiving Day 1952.

THE NP A-4 class locomotives 2670-2677 and the A-5's 2680-2689, built by Baldwin in 1941 and 1943, were considered by many mechanical engineers and students of steam motive power to be the finest examples of Northerns ever built in this country. Both the A-4's and A-5's were 112' 10" long and 16' 4" to the top of the stubby stack, with an imposing 69,800 lbs. of tractive effort on roller bearinged 77" drivers. Both classes were heavy locomotives, weighing, complete with tender, 952,000 lbs. This weight restricted them to main line use where bridges were sturdy enough to bear the load, and their height and wide cabs kept them out of the Cascades and Stampede Tunnel.

The weight factor on the drivers prevented undue slipperiness, even on grades with a heavy train, and made the locomotives exceptionally easy to start. Their fine handling characteristics made the big 2600's at home either in passenger or freight service. The simplicity of line of the all welded centipede tender, the large vestibule cab, and clean small domed boiler, together with the traditional exposed running gear, pumps, graphited smokebox, and unadorned front end combined to make these among the most beautiful steam engines ever built. *Don Roberts*

A PAIR OF OIL BURNING MIKES in pusher service blast their way up South Tacoma hill while helping a drag
bound for the old 'Prairie Line.'

W. Wilkinson

NORTH COAST LIMITED CONNECTION from East Auburn approaches Reservation Tower just outside Tacoma.

Jim Frederickson

A BRACE OF CHALLENGERS hustle an eastbound freight, west of Glendive, Montana.

Jim Frederickson

PUSHER SERVICE on South Tacoma hill!

W. Wilkinson

TIMKEN ENGINE NO. 1111 in St. Paul, January 1932, on the head end of the North Coast Limited.

Bill Converse

PULLMAN STANDARD Motor Car B-23 at South Tacoma as train No. 422 Seattle-Hoquiam local.

Jim Frederickson

EASTBOUND FREIGHT in Stampede Pass, winter of 1967.

Jim Frederickson

MARCH 18, 1940 marked the beginning of the end of steam on the Northern Pacific. EMD (General Motors) #103. 5,400 hp diesel, prototype of the famous FT series, on a trial trip on the head end of the North Coast Limited easily handled the heavy train over the 250 mile distance between Livingston and Missoula, returning that same evening on the eastbound North Coast Limited. No. 2654, a 4500 hp (at 55 mph) 4-8-4 was limited to ten cars on the same run, anything over ten cars required a helper on the 1.8% grade over Bozeman hill.   *W. R. McGee*

EMD #103 races through western Montana on its test run with the North Coast Limited in March 1940.

W. R. McGee

GENERAL MOTORS' "Train of Tomorrow" is on display on NP team track in Seattle, December 10-12, 1947. The "Vista-Dome" equipment was the first seen in the Northwest, and made a deep impression on the then train conscious public. On a nation wide tour during much of 1947, the streamlined equipment, later refurbished and sold to the Union Pacific, was at one time in "pool train" service between Seattle and Portland.   *Jim Frederickson*

NP #408, Seattle to Portland day train starts to accelerate behind a trio of diesel passenger units in A-B-A combination, after passing through the double tracked curved tunnel under the old Tacoma smelter.

Jim Frederickson

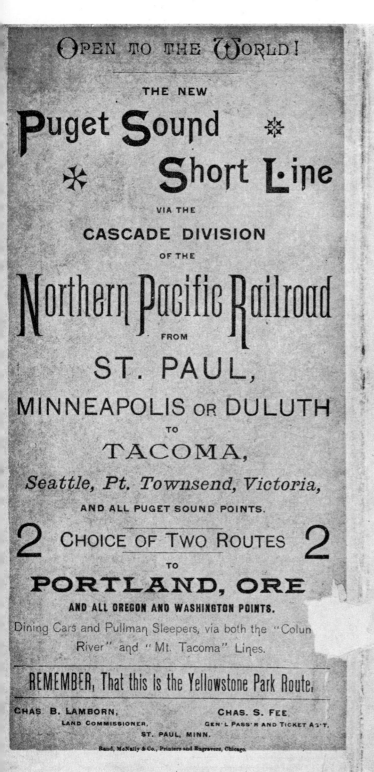

EXCERPTS from two rare N.P. timetables, one from the 1883-1884 and the other from October, 1887, are reproduced on the following pages through the courtesy of Mr. Bill McKenzie of the Public Relations Department of the Northern Pacific Railway. Also reproduced from these time tables is the map of the Northern Pacific which makes up the end papers of this book.

The Northern Pacific Railroad,

AND

THE COUNTRY IT TRAVERSES.

HEN the magnificent country lying between the Great Lakes and the Pacific Ocean, and traversed for 2,000 miles by the Northern Pacific Railroad, is spoken of as "The Wonderland of the World," your mind reverts at once to the matchless scenery of the Bad Lands, the Yellowstone National Park, the Columbia River and Mount Tacoma. But in this remarkable territory, Nature dispenses her bounty with so generous a hand, and the entire region from end to end is so marvelously productive of everything that can contribute to the health, happiness and prosperity of the human race, that were its scenic attractions entirely obliterated, and glacier, geyser and cascade to become things of the past, its wealth-producing possibilities, so vast in their extent, so varied in their character, would still secure for it its well-earned title of "The Wonderland of the World." In other words, the Yellowstone National Park itself, now exciting the interest of the whole world, and universally acknowledged to be without a rival for beautiful, sublime and awe-inspiring scenery, is not one whit more wonderful than the amazing fertility of the soil in almost boundless tracts of country, than the thrift and increase of the cattle on a thousand hills, or the inexhaustible stores of the useful minerals and precious metals that underlie its surface.

THE NORTHERN PACIFIC RAILROAD AND THE GREAT LAKES.

While the Northern Pacific Railroad is especially identified with the great cities of St. Paul and Minneapolis, which owe their commercial importance largely to the development of the country which has been opened up by its construction, and where it receives the bulk of its west-bound traffic—the pleasure-seeking tourist, the enterprising capitalist, and the emigrant filled with bright visions of a prosperity hitherto denied him—it must not be forgotten that it has interests on Lake Superior second only to the foregoing. To three several points, at or near the western extremity of that great lake, does it carry a large share of the teeming produce of its rich territory, and all three, Duluth, Superior City and Ashland, offer great, if not equal, inducements to the enterprising merchant and

manufacturer. First and foremost must be placed Duluth, the most western city on the great chain of North American lakes, and the terminus for various transportation companies, for the facilitating of whose business, with that of the railroad, extensive docks have been constructed and seven mammoth grain elevators erected. This flourishing city, which has now a population of 25,000, contains also numerous saw mills and lumber manufactories, as well as a blast furnace, with a capacity of thirty tons per day. It has its full complement of churches, schools, banks, hotels, newspapers and public halls, and is rapidly progressing toward its manifest destiny as a great commercial city and lake port. At Superior City, Wis., a prosperous and growing town, there are also fine harbor and terminal facilities. At Ashland, Wis., the line connects with

the Wisconsin Central Railroad, running southward to Milwaukee, and the Milwaukee, Lake Shore & Western Railway, whose main line has recently been completed to Ashland. These towns will all attain great commercial importance with the development of the country tributary to the Northern Pacific Railroad, a development of which, notwithstanding the marvelous results that have been attained, we have as yet seen only the beginning.

AGRICULTURAL RESOURCES.

The agricultural resources of the Northern Pacific Country are such as to constitute it a veritable land of promise. Its products vary with the soil and climate, comprising all the innumerable grains and fruits found in the temperate zone. First comes wheat, the king of cereals, the finest variety of which known to commerce, the famous "No. 1 Hard," is the exclusive product of Minnesota and Dakota. This celebrated grade containing an exceptionally large proportion of gluten, makes the best flour in the world, a flour that in turn produces the largest proportionate quantity of the finest bread. It is eagerly sought after by millers and grain buyers in Eastern cities, and it invariably commands from 10 to 15 cents more per bushel than the best grades of other wheat. Furthermore, let it be remembered that nature pours out this treasure without stint—from 20 to 35 bushels to the acre, weighing from 61 to 64 pounds to the bushel, being the average yield. It is only, however, in the Northern Pacific belt that this fine grade of wheat can be raised; the most determined efforts to produce it in other wheat sections of the country, and even in **South Dakota,** having proved **unsuccessful.** The Northern Pacific Railroad has for sale several million acres of land in Minnesota and Dakota that will yield a sure and continuous succession of crops of this famous cereal. Wheat is also cultivated to advantage in the fertile valleys of Montana and on the great plains of Eastern Washington, which latter Territory joins hands with the famous Red River Valley as a wheat-producing district. Although it is the staple product of North Dakota, wheat is by no means the only cereal raised. Oats yield from 60 to 75 bushels per acre, and weigh from 40 to 44 pounds to the bushel, 90 to 100 bushels to the acre being not uncommon. Barley yields 30 to 48 bushels to the acre, weighing from 48 to 54 pounds, and rye 35 to 50 bushels, weighing from 56 to 62 pounds. In limited sections of Montana and extensive tracts in Washington, particularly in the vicinity of Walla Walla and Dayton, these various cereals are raised in the greatest abundance.

Vegetables, comprising all varieties common to the Northern States, are easily raised, yield heavily, grow to great size and are a certain crop. Especially is this the case in Northern Dakota, where potatoes, large in size and uniformly sound and mealy, yield from 150 to 400 bushels to the acre; onions, large and firm, from 400 to 600 bushels to the acre, and turnips, peas, beets, parsnips, carrots, squash, cabbage, cauliflower, egg-plant, lettuce, radishes and melons in like proportion. West of the Rocky Mountains fruits of all kinds, especially apples, plums, pears and grapes, are raised in great profusion, and are noted for size and flavor. Buckwheat, flax, clover, timothy, orchard grass, Hungarian, millet and native grasses of nutritious character, all yield bountiful and profitable crops.

In some parts of Washington, notably in the Puyallup Valley, hop growing is engaged in with great success, the business yielding enormous returns upon the money invested. In this connection it may be stated that dairying is being carried on at various points, with the most satisfactory results, and is likely to become a very important branch of farming industry.

THE GRAZING INDUSTRY.

The enormous impetus given to this industry during the last three years, in North Dakota, west of the Missouri River, and in Eastern Montana, has not only demonstrated beyond all question the remarkable adaptation of this region to grazing purposes, but has made Montana, if not the very first of the States or Territories of the Union, in respect to the actual number of its cattle and sheep, the foremost of them all in regard to the success with which stock raising on a large scale may be conducted. In 1877 Montana contained 220,000 head of cattle and 120,000 sheep. In the succeeding three years the numbers increased to 490,000 cat-

tle and 520,000 sheep, and by the end of 1885 there were 1,000,000 and 975,000 respectively. The grazing interests of the West are steadily moving toward Montana, and vast areas of grazing lands are being taken up. There is scarcely any part of the Territory, excepting upon the mountain ranges, where the climate is not sufficiently mild and the snowfall sufficiently light for cattle to winter out of doors with almost absolute safety. No other food is required during winter than is supplied by the native bunch grass, which cures itself, and stands as hay until the succeeding spring. Cattle fatten upon it more quickly and keep in better condition than those which feed upon the blue grass of Kentucky, or the buffalo grass of Nebraska and Colorado. 85,000 head of cattle were shipped by the Northern Pacific Railroad to Eastern points last year, and they invariably commanded higher market prices than any other cattle. The "Bad Lands," west of the Missouri River, have proved an exceptionally fine region for grazing purposes, and at Medora and other points, extensive abattoirs have been erected by a company, at the head of which is the Marquis de Mores, who has done much to encourage the industry along the line of the railroad. The grazing interest is a large and rapidly growing one, also, in Washington east of the Cascade Range, on the great plains of the Columbia, and the strip of country lying south of the Snake River. In Oregon, also, cattle raising has long been an important industry, second only to that of agriculture. The bunch grasses of the valleys of that State are noted as being among the most luxuriant and nutritious in the West. From 150,000 to 200,000 head of cattle are sold every year in Oregon and Washington for Eastern markets. Sheep husbandry is a great source of profit in Montana, Oregon and Washington. The succulent grasses favor the production of sound, soft wool, without the harshness of that grown in lower latitudes. The profits in this business are very large, as the wool may always be counted upon to return at least 25 per cent. in money on the investment, while the increase in sheep will range from 70 to 90 per cent. per annum. Less capital is required in this business than in cattle raising, and the returns are large and certain. The wool clip of Oregon and Washington, in 1886, was over 19,000,000 pounds. Eligible locations, surrounded by unoccupied areas, eminently suited for pasturing sheep, are still to be found without much expense.

MINERAL RESOURCES.

The Northern Pacific country contains in Montana and Northern Idaho the richest gold and silver bearing region in the world. It seems, indeed, almost like an inversion of the order of nature, that the most productive wheat belt under cultivation should be in such close proximity to the most valuable of all known deposits of the precious metals. Yet, so it is; and that fact, with others herein referred to, explains how it is that the Northern Pacific Railroad is enabled to offer the settler, whether he be a capitalist or one whose means have been exhausted by unsuccessful business operations elsewhere, or who, perhaps, has never before known what it is to have any inducement to industry or providence, advantages and opportunities unequaled in the world. Dakota has an extensive gold-producing region in the Black Hills, the shipments for the year ending June 30, 1884, having been $4,500,000, in addition to a considerable quantity of silver.

The production of gold and silver in Montana has increased from $3,822,379, in 1880, to $23,450,000, in 1885; and the Territory is now at the head of the gold-producing regions of the world. It is a significant fact that its annual yield should show the steady increase it does, when nearly $200,000,000 worth has been taken from its soil. The completion of the Northern Pacific Railroad has stimulated mining enterprises at many points where large bodies of ore are known to exist, and important developments are now in progress in various camps contiguous to the line of railway, and not accessible by any other route. Scarcely less inviting to the prospector and miner, are the comparatively new mining districts of Northern Idaho, in one of which, situated in Kootenai County, 50 miles east of Coeur d'Alene, a vein of free gold, four feet thick, and assaying from $60 to $700 per ton, was recently discovered. The development of the Coeur d'Alene mines has demonstrated the fact that former claims regarding their richness and permanency were well founded, and one of the richest placer mining camps in the world is now beginning to realize the anticipations of two years ago. In addition to gold and silver, Montana and Northern Idaho are especially rich in deposits of copper, lead and iron-bearing ores, tin and other minerals also abounding. In the mountains flanking the Pend d'Oreille River, in Northern Idaho, croppings of heavy lead ores, rich in silver, have been found, and only their inaccessibility has prevented their development. But, that difficulty having been removed by the opening of the railroad, mining operations will no longer be delayed. Gold and silver, with other useful minerals, also exist in large quantities in Washington and Oregon. Over $50,000,000 worth of gold has already been extracted, although only superficial processes have so far been applied. Iron ores of the finest quality are found in large bodies throughout the Pacific Northwest, as are also copper, tin, zinc, lead, plumbago, etc. Great tracts of limestone, building stone and fine pottery clays are found in Montana, and also in Washington and Oregon, where granite and marble also abound. A large portion of the Northwest is underlaid with lignite coal, which is of superior quality and easily worked. It crops out along the bluff ranges on all the streams in Montana for hundreds of miles, in veins of from four to seven feet in thickness. Heavy veins of fine bituminous coal have recently been discovered in the same Territory. An excellent quality of bituminous coal is also found near Tacoma, Roslyn, and at other points in Washington.

LUMBERING, AND THE COLUMBIA RIVER FISHERIES.

Among the important interests of the Pacific Northwest must be mentioned the export trade in lumber and that in canned salmon, the former centering on Puget Sound, and the latter on the Columbia River. The lumber resources of Washington are almost inexhaustible, fully two-thirds of the Territory being covered with forests. The conifers are of great size and height, ranging from eight to fifteen feet in diameter, and from 175 to 350 feet in height. The finest body of timber in the world is embraced between the Columbia River and British Columbia, and the Pacific Ocean and the Cascades. The approximate quantity in the Puget Sound district—nearly as large as the State of Iowa—is 160,000,000,000 feet. The principal growths are fir, pine, spruce, cedar, larch and hemlock, although white oak, maple, cottonwood, ash and other varieties abound. The waters of Oregon and Washington teem with salmon and other varieties of fish of great commercial value, the fisheries constituting in the former State an interest of great importance. Within the last few years, the canning industry has witnessed an astonishing development, the product of the Columbia River alone having, in 1886, reached 620,438 cases, representing, according to the established average, 1,861,314 salmon, weighing 40,948,908 pounds, and valued at $2,750,000.

THE SCENIC WONDERLAND.

In these days of travel, it has become the fashion to bestow, if not upon every particular locality, at least upon nearly every section of country that is not utterly destitute of natural beauty, some high-sounding title or alluring designation. Upon how unsubstantial a foundation not a few of such claims rest, the disappointed traveler need not be told. But no tourist ever returned with unfulfilled expectations from that world of marvels thrown open by the Northern Pacific Railroad; no lover of the beautiful, without unfading impressions, destined to prove an after source of unmingled pleasure and delight; no student of nature, that did not recognize his high privilege in being permitted to gaze upon the most mysterious page in her great book. The country identified with the Northern Pacific Railroad is, from end to end, a distance of 2,000 miles, one of which it is impossible to speak except in superlatives. Entering it at its eastern extremity, the traveler has an opportunity of visiting at Minneapolis the largest flouring mills in the world, in a city that is now the largest primary wheat market in the world; and at Duluth he will gaze, probably for the first time, upon the blue waters of the largest lake in the world. Crossing the Territory of Dakota, he will pass through the greatest wheat farms in the world; and in the Yellowstone National Park he will view with wondering admiration the largest and grandest collection of geysers in the world. On the Columbia River he will see the finest river scenery in the world, surpassing not only that of our own palisaded Hudson, but the beautiful blue Danube, and the castled Rhine; and, lastly, he will find imbedded in the mighty bosom of Mount Tacoma the most magnificent glaciers in the world. These, with countless other attractions for the tourist, the health seeker and the sportsman, are all on the line of the Northern Pacific Railroad. At Detroit, 230 miles from St. Paul, is one of the largest and most beautiful of Minnesota's 10,000 lakes, with the best of fishing, shooting and hotel accommodations. In the far-famed Bad Lands, there is scenery of the most extraordinary character, and an abundance of large game. In addition to the geysers, already referred to, the Yellowstone National Park contains the Falls of the Yellowstone and Gibbon Rivers, the former 350 feet in height, various profound canyons, boiling mud pools, and cliffs of coal-black jet, with the grandest of Rocky Mountain scenery for their background. The Mammoth Hot Springs Hotel, a capacious and admirably appointed caravansary, is only six miles from the terminus of the National Park branch of the railroad. Wagons, saddle horses and guides can be obtained during the season. The traveler to the Pacific Northwest has the choice of the scenery of the peerless Columbia River, or the magnificent views to be had in crossing the Cascade Range; by either route he can visit

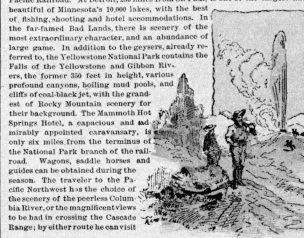

the flourishing city of Portland, and the far-famed Puget Sound. Tacoma, the terminus of the Northern Pacific Railroad on Puget Sound, where one of the finest hotels in the West has recently been opened, is the starting point for Victoria, B. C., a beautiful city, enjoying a delightful climate, in what has well been called "The Florida of the Northwest." The Sound steamers are good, comfortable boats, and they make the trip between Tacoma and Victoria in eight hours. At Tacoma and Victoria connection is made with steamers sailing to Sitka and other points in Alaska, the "Land of the Midnight Sun." The round trip of over 2,000 miles is made in from eleven to eighteen days, almost wholly through inland seas and amid scenery of the most magnificent character, comprising snow-capped mountains, glaciers, icebergs and a thousand and one other features of interest to the student, scientist and pleasure-seeker.

ROAD EQUIPMENT.

The equipment of the Northern Pacific Railroad is such as becomes a road with interests of such magnitude as are those of this great transcontinental line. To begin with, its track is all steel rail and its road-bed solid, thus permitting the greatest speed with perfect safety. Its line is standard gauge throughout, and all its passenger trains are equipped with the Westinghouse Air Brake, Miller Platforms and Patent Steel-Tired Car Wheels. Pullman Palace Drawing Room Sleeping Cars, of the latest and most improved pattern, run between St. Paul and Tacoma and Portland. In these Sleepers elegance, comfort, neatness, convenience and safety are all combined. Passengers desiring berths reserved in the Pullman Sleeping Cars on the Northern Pacific Railroad, can secure them by applying to the conductor of the train on which they enter St. Paul or Minneapolis, who will telegraph to the ticket agents in advance. Not only is the Northern Pacific the only line running Dining Cars between St. Paul and Minneapolis and Fargo, Moorhead and other points in the famous Red River Valley, but it is also the only transcontinental line running any

form of Dining Cars between the East and Portland, Oregon, Tacoma, W. T., and other Pacific Coast points. Its Dining Cars, which were built at the Pullman Car Works, are marvels of luxury, being of the most elegant design and finish. They are mounted on combination springs, so carefully adjusted that not the least jar disturbs the elegantly appointed tables. In these cars the passenger sits down to a bountiful "spread," comprising all the delicacies in season on both the Atlantic and Pacific Coasts, as well as fish and game obtained from the country through which the road passes. The cars are under the direct supervision of one of the most experienced caterers in the country. Meals are furnished at only 75 cents each, and are served with promptness, the attention given to the wants of all patrons being equal to that of any hotel in the land. Passengers not desiring a regular meal, will be furnished from the Dining Car with lunches, at reasonable prices. The ordinary first class coaches are newly built, and among the best ever manufactured by the Pullman Car Company. Second-class passengers ride in good, clean coaches, on the same train as first-class passengers.

Emigrant Sleepers are run on express trains between St. Paul and Portland, and during the night ride over the Cascade Division. No other line runs Emigrant Sleepers, or any other kind of emigrant cars into Montana or Washington Territories. These cars are fitted with berths similar to those in first-class sleepers, the only material difference being that the berths in the former are not upholstered. No extra charge is made for berths in these sleepers, but passengers must furnish their own blankets and such other bedding as they may desire. At the news-stand in the Union Depot, St. Paul, and on all passenger trains going east or west, emigrants can purchase single tufted tick mattresses for $1.90 each; pillows at 25 cents each, and a pair of single blankets, including shawl strap, for $1.50. It is not necessary to travel in an emigrant sleeper to appreciate the value of these accommodations to those for whose comfort they have been provided.

ESE CELEBRATED SLEEPING CARS ARE RUN THROUGH BETWEEN ST. PAUL AND PORTLAND, OREGON

...ior View of the New Pullman Palace Sleeping Cars now Running on the Northern Pacific R. R. through between St. Paul and Portland.

(See another page for more about these Cars, rates, etc.)

From 1883 NP Timetable

Cover of 1883 Timetable

Reprinted from 1883 Timetable

207

A PAIR OF ALCO HELPERS push with all their 3,000 horsepower on the rear of a westbound freight as it ascends the first stiff grade up into the Rockies just west of Livingston, Montana.

Jim Frederickson